MW01222569

Blessings

+ GW

Christ
&
Caribbean Culture(s)

Christ
&
Caribbean Culture(s)

A Collection of Essays on Caribbean Christology
and Its Pastoral Implications

By

Gabriel Malzaire

authorHOUSE®

AuthorHouse™
1663 Liberty Drive
Bloomington, IN 47403
www.authorhouse.com
Phone: 1 (800) 839-8640

Published by AuthorHouse 06/30/2015

ISBN: 978-1-5049-2003-2 (sc)
ISBN: 978-1-5049-2004-9 (e)

Library of Congress Control Number: 2015910329

Print information available on the last page.

This book is printed on acid-free paper.

Scripture quotations marked JB are from The Jerusalem Bible, copyright © 1966 by Darton, Longman & Todd, Ltd. and Doubleday, a division of Bantam Doubleday Dell Publishing Group, Inc. Reprinted by permission.

DEDICATION

In this the thirtieth year of my ordination to the Holy Priesthood, I dedicate this publication to my deceased parents, Joseph Edison Malzaire & Oliver Malzaire, and also the parishioners of Mon Repos, Saint Lucia, who were instrumental in nurturing my vocation.

TABLE OF CONTENTS

FOREWORD

"Who is the Caribbean man?" This was the overriding question posed to participants of the Antilles Pastoral Institute (API) of the 1970s which was sponsored by the Antilles Episcopal Conference. This yearly gathering, conducted jointly by the Catechetical Centres of the Archdioceses of Kingston and Port of Spain, was undoubtedly a valuable workshop dealing with inculturation and evangelisation specifically mounted for catechists and foreign missionaries working in the Caribbean. Unfortunately, it fizzled out for lack of any sustained exegesis other than that furthered by sociology which was fired by the then popular Black Power movement. Notwithstanding the demise of the API, the question is still relevant: "Who is the Caribbean person?"

The Caribbean person cannot only be identified by mere sociological understanding or exegesis whose sole objective is one of liberation from external colonial forces that forged—first, ever so brutally—the commingling of the various cultures in the Caribbean, which makes us unique. Rather, from a cultural and religious perspective, we begin to understand better the quest of the Caribbean person which is one of genuine freedom and liberation.

This is theologically pursued by Bishop Gabriel Malzaire in this short presentation, *Christ and Caribbean Culture(s)*. He proposes that the identity crisis will forever remain a crisis if we do not see humanity through the prism of Christ, the God-Man who assumed—nay, married—our humanity so that we may be the Christ incarnate in today's world. This is a welcome reminder couched in theological terms with a wide range of references throughout, including Second Vatican Council documents and various authors: the great liberation theologian, Gustavo Guttierez of Latin America; Idris Hamid and Clifford F. Payne of the Caribbean; spiritual writer, Henri Nouwen; Martin Luther King, Jr. and other Afro-Americans from North America.

At this juncture of our Caribbean history when the northern metropolis tends to mesmerize our identity-confused people with post-modern concepts of the human person, the reflections articulated in these pages invite every serious reader to ponder. They challenge us to acknowledge, accept, and come to grips not only with the baggage of cruel slavery and indentureship, but more so with the unique richness which we, as a truly Caribbean people, have by virtue of the Incarnation of the Virgin-Born. The historical Jesus, inculturated in his Palestinian culture, is the pattern which God, our Father, uses to cast the mould for everyone, be s/he Black, White, Indian, Chinese, or Arab—all intermingling, somewhat painfully, to bring about a particular people who belong to and are loved by God. Notwithstanding the presence of such differing ethnicities, the author essays to lay the ground work for a Christian civilisation within the Caribbean Region.

Effecting such a Christian civilisation entails, at the outset, the acknowledgement of our Caribbean realities which are hurdles to be faced by a Church called to be dialogic and ecumenical, compassionate and prophetic. Without these ecclesial qualities and the acknowledgement and "owning" of our Caribbean realities, there can be no forward movement towards true liberation and the realisation of the Christian civilisation envisioned. The author reminds his readers that liberation is "a continuous process of maturation to bring ourselves as a people to a more wholesome sense of our humanity." In this process, morality, which is the "cutting edge of theology," cannot be ignored or hijacked by a simplistic personal salvation palliative. Nor can it be sugar-coated by the post-modern "values" of relativism and the struggle for human rights without responsibility towards the integrity of creation and the common good. Walking through these pages and reflecting upon the truths therein, perhaps we may be better able to grasp with clarity the perennial question: "Who is the Caribbean person?"

+Donald J. Reece, D.D.
Archbishop Emeritus of Kingston

PREFACE

During graduate studies in Missiology at the Catholic Theological Union in Chicago (1987-1989), I was deeply inspired by Professor Robert J. Schreiter through his course entitled *Constructing Local Theologies*. This led me to begin exploring theological themes within the context of the Caribbean. Consequently, my MA Thesis was entitled *Contextual Ecclesiology - A Study of the Basic Ecclesial Community as a Model for Caribbean Ecclesiology*, which was directed by Professor Schreiter.

From the post-Vatican II period, the Caribbean Church, like many others, has been exploring the means of inculturating the Gospel message in the local situations in which it is called to serve. In other words, there was a thrust towards *contextuality*; Church leaders and theologians were seeking to articulate the faith in the setting of the local Church.

In the Caribbean, this quest for localness in theology and ecclesiology found expression among its budding theologians through the establishment of the Caribbean Theological Conference, the first of which took place in St. Lucia in June, 1994. In fact, Part III of this publication is part of the proceeds of that conference. This forum among Caribbean theologians has provided the avenue for much research and discussion on the Caribbean theological and ecclesial reality.

It is fitting, therefore, to say that this publication has been inspired by that movement of theological reflection on the Caribbean reality in formal studies and through theological conferences. Additionally, having been a columnist of the Archdiocesan Newspaper in St. Lucia, *The Catholic Chronicle*, also provided an avenue for theological discussion and exposition.

It is my hope that this small collection will provide readers with insights into the theological issues with which we grapple, sometimes without realizing it. I trust that it will be a source of deeper reflection on those themes, and will be an impetus for appropriate pastoral action.

ACKNOWLEDGEMENTS

This small corpus brings together four essays which I have presented over the last two decades with special focus on the Caribbean theological and ecclesial reality. Despite them having been exposed to one forum or another, I express heartfelt thanks to various persons for their contributions to its presentation in this present form.

First I express my deep appreciation to Archbishop Donald Reece, Archbishop Emeritus of Kingston in Jamaica, for presenting the Foreword to this publication. His long experience of the Caribbean Church no doubt brought richness to his comments on the text and his positive advice towards the final work.

Sincere gratitude to Fr. Nigel Karam, a priest of the Diocese of Roseau, who is presently pursuing doctoral studies with the University of St. Thomas Aquinas in Rome. His editorial suggestions were most thorough and encouraging. If I had any doubt about the credibility of this collection, his personal endorsement of the content was reason to proceed with the project.

Gabriel Malzaire

Dr. Lennox Honeychurch, though not a theologian, his expertise as one of the leading historians in the Caribbean, assisted in the verification of the historical accuracy of parts of the material presented and comments on the general tenor of the book. For this I am deeply thankful.

Finally, I owe a debt of gratitude to various persons such as Msgr. Patrick A. B. Anthony, Archbishop Joseph Harris, CSSp, Fr. Michel de Verteuil, CSSp., Bishop Jason Gordon, Fr. Henry Charles, Dr. Everard Johnston, Dr. Gerard Boodoo, and other participants of the Caribbean Theology Conference who, over the last two decades, have stimulated theological reflection on the Caribbean ecclesial reality to engender proper pastoral action.

GENERAL INTRODUCTION

This short publication is a collection of essays which have been presented at various fora over the last two decades, namely, the Caribbean Theological Conference, a gathering of the Living Water Community in Trinidad and the Catholic Chronicle Newspaper of the Archdiocese of Castries, Saint Lucia. They focus specifically on the Caribbean Church in its quest to make sense of its experience of being Church in its particular context. Living up to the dictum that theology is *faith seeking understanding*, this collection provides reflections on some aspects of the lived faith experiences of the Caribbean people and also articulates, hopefully in an understandable manner, aspects that many members of the Church do not normally think about for one reason or another.

Part I: *The Challenges for the Catholic Christian in the New Millennium* articulates the major preoccupation of the Caribbean Church, as in many other parts of the world. These are discussed under three main themes, namely: *relevance, authenticity* and *evangelization*. The section presents these themes as areas which do, and ought to engage the Church's hierarchy and every individual Catholic Christian in the Caribbean, who are concerned about the appropriate evangelical posture for the contemporary period.

Part II: *Christ and Ethnicity in the Caribbean* is an attempt, through the use of the notion of the Incarnation, to unravel the concept of Christ as Saviour in the context of the Caribbean as a people with a unique history. It attempts to show that genuine Caribbean theology is a reflection on the Christ-Event in the lives of its people. It is geared towards helping Christians in the Caribbean develop a greater sense of self-worth as a people being saved. Moreover, it brings to the fore the fact that Christology must be related to the identity of a people if it is to engender appropriate and effective pastoral action.

Pat III: *Towards a Caribbean Christian Civilization* gives a panoramic and comprehensive view of the Caribbean reality in which Christianity is being lived. It takes into consideration the influence of the history of the region, the effects of colonialism, the evolution of its culture(s), its ethnic composition and the attitudes and dispositions that surrounded it, the challenge of traditional religious elements, and the moral question in its varied dimensions. In the end, this section presents some suggestions on what a Caribbean Christian civilization should look like if it is to carry out the mandate of Christ to His Church.

A short *Theological Reflection on "Bamboo Bursting" in the Caribbean* serves as a postscript to the text. It unravels the meaning of this pre-Christmas past-time in some of the territories of the Caribbean.

Short though it may be, the collection provides a fair grasp of the Caribbean Church's experience and the responsibility we have to make it what it ought to be - a leaven in the midst of God's people in context.

PART I

The Challenges for the Catholic Christian in the New Millennium

Introduction

In the advent of the Second Vatican Council the problems which faced the Church could be summed up into four key issues around which the Council was convened. They were: the question of the Church's relevance in the modern world; the question of unity among Christians; the reality of dispiritedness in the Church; and the Church's need for internal reform.

Fifty years later, we ask ourselves whether some of the same needs recur in the very fabric of the Church in the new millennium. My suspicion is that all the above remain, to a significant extent, part of the description of the present reality. However, I propose to elucidate the theme under three related headings:

1. The first remains the same as that which concerned the Council Fathers fifty years ago—the question of the relevance of the Church's message in the present age and how Catholic Christians today rise to the challenge;

2. The second concerns the challenge to authenticity in the Church's mission to the present age; and

3. The third involves the question of how the Church lives up to her mandate to evangelise.

1. Relevance

Throughout the history of Christianity the evangelical and pastoral relevance of the Church have always been judged by her effectiveness in the world. Her very credibility is not solely dependent on any view or perception. However, the efficacy of her mission in the world also includes the extent to which her message reaches the needs, aspirations, hopes, fears of the faithful whom she is called to serve.

A few decades ago it seemed easier to be a Catholic Christian in the Caribbean, and maybe in the world at large. People pledged their loyalty to the Church without much difficulty. They followed the leadership entrusted to them without much question. In those days the hub of both religious and social life of the community was around the parish Church. There existed a close marriage between Church and State. The Church played a key role in the area of education of the nation, and therefore, such a position of influence rendered it possible and maybe easy for evangelization and the retention of its members. The reality today is vastly different. In many of our Catholic Schools a significant percentage of their enrolment comprise non-Catholics, non-Christians and even those who have no particular religious affiliation. The Church in many Caribbean territories, therefore, has been thrust from a position of considerable power and influence into a world environment where pluralism is the order of the day. She exists in a world characterised by a diversity of views and opinions on any given reality, whether spiritual or otherwise. Moreover, with the availability of modern communication technology, everyone, whether rich and not so rich, is exposed to these diverse ways of perceiving the world. People possess the freedom to choose the manner in which they wish to exist in it and this includes their perception of the role the Church plays in their lives.

In the modern age, no longer do people follow the faith because the priest (the man of God) says so. What is believed has to make sense to them. It must substantially add something to their lives, especially since the truth that the Church speaks today can be judged against other interpretations of that truth. More than ever before, Catholic theology is being forcefully influenced by a growing fundamentalist trend, even to the extent that their methods and practices are infiltrating Catholic mode of worship and the use of the Holy Scriptures. It seems to me that there is a rapid shift from the appreciation of what was mysterious, and therefore deemed holy in the past, to what is tangible and accessible today. The Church in the Caribbean has a real experience of this reality.

The danger of this sometimes superficial manner of determining what are considered the needs of the modern times is that we can limit ourselves to what is appealing to the senses and that which brings immediate satisfaction, over and against the quest for the kind of depth that would be more long lasting, and which seems more consonant with the normal human-spiritual development. We live in an age of a quick-fix mentality, which is often more attractive than the laborious search for spiritual depth.

However, it is in the midst of all these conditions, that the Church is challenged to constantly ask herself how relevant she is to the times in which she exists. In this new millennium it becomes an even more pertinent matter of concern. The analysts of the pre-Vatican II period had concluded that the external decline in the Church was matched by an internal one. The present reality is that more and more nominal Catholics as well as active ones are giving up the practice of the faith, especially in situations where the environmental and religious pressures on them to remain loyal are weakening. No longer are people willing to follow the dictates of the Church out of habit. The atmosphere is such that whatever they choose to put their faith in has to be the result of a conviction. No longer are they ready to follow the rule out of fear. Instead, more people are seeking to arrive at rational choices that benefit their lives. The Church has to rise to these prevailing needs in the lives of the faithful. In other words, She has to be relevant to the needs that arise in accordance with the times in which we live.

However, there is another side to the issue of relevance. Henri Nouwen, a prolific American spiritual writer, sees the challenge of being relevant as a temptation to the modern Church leader. From his experience of living in a community of mentally handicapped persons, he came to realise that all the successes of his earlier life were of little significance in comparison to the task of being an instrument of salvation in the modern world. He came to the conclusion that "the Christian leader of the future is called to be completely irrelevant and to stand in this world with nothing to offer but his or her own vulnerable self."[1] He maintains that it is so because "this is the way Jesus came to reveal God's love."[2]

Nouwen reminds us that "Jesus' first temptation was to be relevant; to turn stones into bread."[3] It is without doubt a temptation of every minister of religion to take the short cut in their quest to save the masses.

---

[1] Henri Mouwen, *In the Name of Jesus, Reflections on Christian Leadership*, Darton, Longman & Todd, 1989, 17.

[2] Ibid., 17.

[3] Ibid., 17.

7

This is especially so in a growing secular environment, in which the Christian leader feels less significant and more sidelined. Nouwen maintains that "beneath all the great accomplishments of our time, there is a deep current of despair. While efficiency and control are the great aspirations of our society, the loneliness, isolation, lack of friendship and intimacy, broken relationships, boredom, feelings of emptiness and depression, and a deep sense of uselessness fill the hearts of millions of people in our success-oriented world."[4]

Nouwen quotes Bret Easton Ellis in his novel *Less Than Zero*, in which he gives a most vivid account of the moral and spiritual deficiencies responsible for the modern disguise of affluence, accomplishment, admiration of the public and the sense of control over life. He describes the licentiousness and dangerous lifestyle among the youth of the affluent performers of the big city. "The cry that arises from behind all this decadence is clearly: Is there anybody who loves me; is there anybody who really cares? Is there anybody who wants to stay home for me? Is there anybody who wants to be with me when I am not in control, when I feel like crying? Is there anybody who can hold me and give me a sense of belonging?"[5] He affirms

---

4   Ibid., 20-21.

5   Ibid., 21-22.

that "feeling irrelevant is a much more general experience than we might think when we look at the seemingly self-confident society."[6]

He concludes by affirming that "the leader of the future will be the one who dares to claim his irrelevance in the contemporary world as a divine vocation that allows him or her to enter into a deep solidarity with the anguish underlying all the glitter of success and to bring the light of Jesus there."[7] This is the challenge of the Church in the new millennium. This is the challenge of the Church in the Caribbean.

2. Authenticity

The question of authenticity that the Church faces in the new millennium has to do with the quality of its imaging of the one for whom it exists—Jesus Christ. The question is: how is the Church able to live authentically in these modern times the values that characterised the mission of Jesus Christ? It asks in essence: how can we, her members, be true ambassadors for Christ in the world today?

---

6   Ibid., 22.

7   Ibid., 22.

This demands continuous reflection on the more important elements of the salvific mission of Jesus, as reflected in the gospels, notwithstanding the differences in culture and epoch. This necessitates the constant reading of the signs of the times. Thus, an issue such as the growing poverty in the world and how it impinges on the practice of faith is no doubt a significant place to begin.

We live in a time of heightened thirst for spirituality on the one hand, and an age of growing indifference to the church and atheistic tendencies on the other. As regards the former, it is often primarily a quest for personal spiritual fulfillment without necessarily a well-integrated social dimension. Thus, the Christian call to sanctity is perceived as an invitation to intensify one's life of prayer by focusing on a personal relationship with God and Jesus. We are all familiar with the contemporary adage: *"accept Jesus as your Lord and personal saviour."* The problem with this is that it sometimes gives the impression that once the Christian's relationship with the heavens is in place, all is well. The horizontal dimension, which involves interpersonal relationships and relationships with the things from below are judged secondary. It is not surprising that our sense of stewardship regarding the things of the earth is not often considered a moral responsibility. Problems such as pollution, deforestation, exploitation of the earth's resources are too remote from our religious consciences, despite adverse consequences.

To my mind, a quest for spirituality without a corresponding awareness of social needs is wanting and sometimes even empty. We know the saying *"too much work without play makes Jack a dull boy."* The same applies conversely: *"too much play without work still makes Jill a dull girl."* This simply means that we cannot play the spiritual game without backing it up with some social action. The truly spiritual person is the one who seeks to integrate the three inseparable dimensions of human existence. He/she has a vital vertical relationship, is in touch with self, and has a healthy disposition towards the external world. We hear the voice of St. James in his epistle saying that *"pure unspoilt religion, in the eyes of God our Father is this: coming to the help of the orphans and widows when they need it, and keeping oneself uncontaminated by the world"* (James 1: 27). He sums up this position a little later by asserting that *"faith without deeds is useless"* (James 2:20). It seems, therefore, that the credibility of the Church's mission rests on how well She responds to those who are in greatest need in our societies.

The notion of poverty has diverse connotations in the Caribbean and in the world at large; and so it is well for Christians to seek comprehension of these varied implications and manifestations today. In a general sense we can say that the poor are those who are in any kind of need; those who suffer any kind of deprivation, oppression or injustice. In the present age this would include women, children, and workers unjustly treated. Since the early 1960s the French theologian Jean Daniélou stated that *"the liturgy will not be fully effective in the Church and in the world, if the poor are continuously neglected."*[8] Therefore he sees care for the poor as an indispensable dimension in the realisation of the eucharistic mission of the Church. Here again the emphasis is on the necessary equilibrium demanded between the vertical and horizontal dimensions of the Christian life.

The Second Vatican Council in its Pastoral Constitution on the Church in the Modern World, (*Gaudium et spes*), states in its opening paragraph: *"The joy and hope, the grief and anguish of the men of our time, especially those of the poor or afflicted in any way, are the joy and hope, the grief and anguish of the followers of Christ as well"* (*GS.* 1). Again in its Dogmatic Constitution on the Church (*Lumen Gentium*), it also states forcefully that *"Just as Christ carried out the work of redemption in poverty and oppression, so the Church is called to follow the*

---

[8]   Jean Daniélou, *Prayer as a Political Problem*, London 1967, 16.

same path if she is to communicate the fruits of salvation to humanity" (*LG.* 8). Here lies one of the greatest challenges of the mission of the Church in the new millennium – its radical identification with the poor in a way that Jesus did.

This is not meant necessarily to make some people feel guilty about their state of life. However, I think the more pertinent question to ask is: to what extent is the Church in the new millennium at the service of the world, and by extension, the individual Catholic Christian? My understanding of the poverty to which the Church is called is not limited simply to what She has or doesn't have, but rather refers more profoundly to the quality of service that She is capable of offering to the world with the gifts that are at her disposal, be they spiritual or otherwise. Thus, the same applies to the individual Christian. Just as Jesus said that *"the Son of Man did not come to be served but to serve and to give his life as a ransom for many"* (Mk 10:45), this ought to be the disposition of the Church. Her service has, of necessity, to do with her capacity for compassion—the same compassion the Jesus showed. In this new millennium the challenge before us is to become a gentler, more compassionate Church; forging new means of liberation and freedom for humanity, and to be experienced as a true life-giver.

3. Evangelisation

All that has been said in the forgoing paragraphs, we could say, meet under the overarching mandate given to the Church to evangelise the world. Since the opening of the New Millennium, the Holy Father has been calling all Catholic Christians to a new evangelical thrust. Traditionally we have viewed the work of evangelisation as something proper to the "priest and them;" and the "them" are the nuns. This ought not to be so! The gospel mandate is one directed to the whole ecclesial body. Every Catholic Christian is to realise that he/she has a specific part to play in the advancement of the kingdom in a way that nobody else can, since we bring to it our uniqueness and our gifts.

But the task of evangelisation is not to be perceived simply as preaching the word. It must be accompanied by Christian witness. In fact, people of this age are more attracted to a life lived rather than to those who become experts in preaching the word.[9] This reminds me of a line in a poem I learnt some years ago during a morning assembly at an infant school on the island of Bimini in the Bahamas. It went like this: *"I would rather see a sermon any day than to hear one."* On hearing this line, I was struck by its deep implications for what I perceive to be demanded of the

---

[9]   Cf. PAUL VI, *Evangelii Nuntiandi* 41.

evangelising mission of the Church in the new millennium. It tells us that if every Catholic Christian becomes a true witness to the gospel message there would be less need for all the ineffective speeches that we so often give.

As regards the presentation of the word, we can easily be attracted to the gimmicks rather than the essence of the message. From a psychological point of view, I am not indicating that the means and method of presenting the word do not help its receptivity. In fact, the Holy Father, Pope John Paul II constantly encouraged the Church to maximise its use of the modern means of social communication to facilitate the presentation of the word and to increase its scope. However, never should we lose sight of the fact that the fruit of true evangelisation is the conversion to Christ, the attainment of freedom, and the possibility of full life for all. This is best attained through the encouragement of a living witness. Jesus himself puts it very simply when he said to his followers that "*they will know that you are my disciples by the love you have one for another*" (Jn. 13:35). It is the civilization of love which Pope Paul VI spoke of as early as the 1960s and 1970s. It still remains for us a challenge in the third millennium.

Lenten Sermon, Living Water Community
April 2, 2001

PART II

Christ and Ethnicity
in the Caribbean

Introduction

The question of a relationship between ethnicity and Christology[10] is by no means a rhetorical one. It is a question deeply rooted in the meaning and significance of the person of Jesus Christ to the various cultures of humanity. Once a people begin to discover their identity in him then they find it necessary to articulate their understanding of faith in him using expressions particular to them. Given the necessity for constant theological reflection, the importance of this question becomes real for us in the Caribbean. First, I present a brief sketch of some of the approaches to the Christological question as conceived in the earlier periods of Christian history.

Early Responses to the Christological Question

Up until the end of the eighteenth century, the traditional approach to Christiology began by acknowledging the universal significance of the Christ-Event as defined by the early councils of Nicea (325), Ephesius (431) and finally, Chalcedon (451). It affirms that "Christ is a divine person with two natures - a human nature and a divine nature …. It starts with God and then

---

[10] The field of study within Christian Theology which is primarily concerned with the nature and person of Jesus as recorded in the canonical Gospels and the Epistles of the New Testament.

goes to affirm how the eternal Son became man."[11] By
the end of the eighteenth century there began a different
view of the Gospel account of Jesus' life, death and
resurrection. Before then "it was generally assumed that
the New Testament gave a clear and accurate account of
the life of the historical Jesus. It was also taken for granted
that the proclaimed Christ and Lord of the early Church
was a replica of the earthly Jesus."[12] But it is clear that
when one turns to the Gospels he discovers that they do
not give us a historical account strictly speaking, of the
life of Jesus in terms of providing a chronological record of
what happened. Instead the Gospels present us primarily
with a faith-picture of the early Church's experience and
understanding of Jesus who is the Christ and the risen
Lord.[13]

We know that each of the four Gospels is different
because of the varied circumstances in which they
were written; each reflecting the concerns of different
communities. Paul too had a different Christology based
on his unique experience of Christ. Stephen Sykes is quoted
as saying that "the Christian message itself contains a

[11] Jon Sobrino, S.J., *Christology at the Crossroads*, Orbis Books,
Maryknoll, New York, 1987, 3-4

[12] Dermot A. Lane, *The Reality of Jesus*, Paulist Press, New York,
N.Y., 1975, 20.

[13] Cf. Ibid., 19.

basic ambiguity that makes pluralism and controversy part of the identity or essence of Christianity itself."[14]

The late nineteenth and early twentieth century European theologians attest to the truth of this statement in the Christological debates which characterised that period. The first was Herman S. Ramarus, a German professor, who claimed that the Gospel accounts had smothered the life of the historical Jesus in supernatural dogma. From this he initiated a quest from the Christ of dogma to the real Jesus. It proved to be a failure. Albert Schweitzer subsequently took it up and embarked on a new quest for the historical Jesus. He too did not get very far with his investigations. Then came Rudolph Bultmann with the claim that "the most we can know with absolute certainty about the historical Jesus is that he existed and that he died on a cross."[15] Some other theologians, referred to as the Post-Bultmannians, arose in the early 1950's and re-addressed the question of the historical Jesus in what was called a "New Quest." They were followed by Wolfhart Pannenberg and his followers of the mid-1960s who disagreed with the Post-Bultmannians on matters relating to the Christ-Event.

[14] Stephen B. Bevans, *Models of Contextual Theology*, Orbis Books, Maryknoll, New York, 1994, 3, quoting Stephen Sykes, *The Identity of Christianity*, London: SPCK, 1984, 23.

[15] Ibid., 22.

According to Dermot Lane, the benefit of this sort of survey of the quest for the historical Jesus is that it opens up for us some of the issues involved in trying to get back to the historical foundations of the Christ-Event.[16] It gives a point of reference in conceptualising the varied Christologies that are prevalent today. This is because the starting point of understanding Christ is the historical Jesus, that is, the person, teaching, attitudes and the deeds of Jesus of Nazareth. In other words, the object of Christian faith is not Christology, but Jesus himself, which means that the task of Christology is to bring greater congruence between the Jesus of history and the Christ of faith. Gustavo Gutierrez urges interest in the historical Jesus when he says, "To approach the man Jesus of Nazareth, in whom God was made flesh, to penetrate not only in his teaching, but also in his life, what it is that gives his word an immediate, concrete context, is a task which more and more needs to be undertaken."[17]

Aaron Parker, in his reflection on *The Nature of Christ in the Black Church*, tells us that "it is accurate to state that black Church persons tend to move beyond questions concerning the co-existence of the divine and human natures of Jesus Christ, even though many black

---

[16] Ibid., 23.

[17] John Sobrino, S.J., *Christology at the Crossroads*, 11.

Christians tacitly accept the conclusions of Chalcedon. Instead they want to know what Jesus had done, is doing, and will do in the personal and social lives of those he has touched. Thus the black Church approaches Christology from a historical and soteriological[18] vantage point; its basic concern lies in Jesus' action in first century Palestine and the implications of these actions for our present and future salvation."[19] James Cone also, made an emphatic contribution to that thought. He states that "we (black theologians) want to know who Jesus was because we believe that is the only way to assess who he is. If we have no historical information about the character and behaviour of that particular Galilean in the first century, then it is impossible to determine the mode of his existence now. Without some continuity between the historical Jesus and the Kerygmatic[20] Christ, the Christian Gospel becomes nothing but the subjective reflection of the early Christian community."[21]

---

[18] Regarding the study of the religious doctrine of salvation.

[19] Aaron L. Parker, *Theological Perspectives of the Nature of Jesus Christ in the Black Church*, University Microfilm, International, Ann Arbor, Michigan, 1987, 15.

[20] A Greek word used in the New Testament for "preaching," hence the Christ preached.

[21] Aaron L. Parker, *Theological Perspectives of the Nature of Jesus Christ in the Black Church*, University Microfilm, International, Ann Arbor, Michigan, 1987, 18.

What comes to the fore very clearly is the importance of "context" as the matrix for doing theology. Therefore, it seems proper to conclude that Christology today is dependent on our perception of the historical Jesus vis-a-vis the reality of the faith experience of the people involved. From this point of view, we can conceive of a Christology that would be meaningful to the Caribbean experience. I propose to elaborate on this concept by looking at the implications of the mystery of the Incarnation.

The Incarnation and Understanding the Christ-Event

The realisation of salvation in the Christian order is rooted in the fact that God entered human history in the person of Jesus, and through his life, death and resurrection brought to humanity the unique possibility of experiencing life to the fullest. This coming together of God and humankind in Jesus is known as the Incarnation. Lane explains it as that which happens through the grace of the self-descending communication of God reaching and touching the self-ascending transcendent being of humankind.[22] Put another way, he says that, "this profound mystery of 'God made man' is to say that the fullest and most organic integration of Godhead and manhood …. has taken place in Jesus of Nazareth."[23]

---

[22] Cf. Dermot A. Lane, *The Reality of Jesus*, 1975, 130-131.

[23] Dermot A. Lane, *The Reality of Jesus*, 1975, 131.

The belief in the Incarnation brings us right back to the reality of the historical Jesus. The experience of the apostles and other persons of faith in this encounter were such that they could testify upon reflection that they had seen and touched God in human form. The belief in this experience of Jesus by the apostles was retained in dogmatic formulations to affirm the humanity and divinity of Jesus. However, "the reality of the Incarnation is a mystery that was present throughout the life of Jesus which like the divinity was only progressively disclosed to the apostles in their experience and reflection upon his life, death and resurrection."[24]

It becomes clear that the affirmation of Genesis 1:27 (the creation of human beings in the image and likeness of God) has no substance outside the reality of the Incarnation, in which it finds its full meaning. "The goal of creation is incarnation so that in a real sense creation reaches its point of completion in and through the reality of the Incarnation."[25] This is to say that human persons can reach their fullest potential only because God identifies with the human cause in the Incarnation. As the Second Vatican Council Document puts it, "He who is the 'image of the invisible God' is himself the perfect man who has

---

[24] Ibid., 133.

[25] Ibid., 134.

restored in the children of Adam that likeness of God which has been disfigured ever since by sin."[26] Therefore, who we are as persons, as believers in the person of Jesus, is who we are as persons in whom Christ is incarnated or progressively being incarnated. Karl Rahner asserts that "because of the Incarnation God is in humankind and remains so for all eternity, and humankind is for all eternity the expression of the mystery of God because the whole human race has been assumed in the individual reality of Jesus."[27] Incarnation entails the taking of the shape and form, and entering into the life of the other in the profoundest of ways possible. Stephen Bevans refers to it as "a process of becoming particular,"[28] meaning, its situatedness in a particular culture. Therefore, we cannot speak of incarnation unless God takes the features of the participants in this incarnational process. Therein lies the basis of the question of the relationship between ethnicity and Christology. This realisation does something, I think, to the dignity of the individual person and of groups of people. It leads one to the affirmation that my Saviour-

---

[26] Austin Flannery, "*Gaudium es Spes* #22, *Documents of Vatican II*, Costello Publishing Company, Northport, New York, 922.

[27] Richard P. McBrian, (ed.), "Current and Recent Catholic Christology" by Karl Rahner, *Catholicism*, Western Press Inc. 430 Oak Grove, Minneapolis, MN, 1970, 477.

[28] Stephen B. Bevans, *Models of Contextual Theology*, Orbis Books, Maryknoll, 1994, 8.

God "looks like me." In other words, it is the realisation that indeed God has become one of us in the person Jesus - He is Emmanuel—God-With-Us. This is essentially the meaning to John 1:14: *"The Word was made flesh and lived among us."*

The Incarnation, the Reality of Christ and Ethnicity

The entire Christological enterprise boils down to one basic question: Who is Jesus Christ for us today? Edward Schillebeeckx provides us with some insight into this answer when he asserts:

> The question emerging from this potted survey of Jesus images, … is whether all these Christological patterns are pure projections of our own, time and time prevailing, increasingly changing interpretation of reality. Once somebody has discovered final salvation in Jesus, it is natural (and proper) that he should project his own expectations and ways of envisaging the "true being" of man onto Jesus."[29]

The change or stability of the image of Jesus perceived by persons is generally dependent on the context of their life situations. What Jesus Christ means to us would simply beg the question, how can he bring salvation, healing and wholeness to our particular situation. The

---

[29] Edward Schillebeeckx, *Jesus: An Experiment of Christology*, Crossroads, New York, 1987, 65.

focus on the social context means that we cannot separate the question about Jesus from the concreteness of everyday life. In fact any christological exposition which denies or is completely silent about the social implications of Jesus Christ's saving work misunderstands or displaces what was central to Jesus' proclamation and practice, namely the Kingdom of God. The variance in socio-historical experience of a people, therefore, has something to do with their perception of Christ as saviour in their lives. Consequently, the Christology of the person in Asia or Australia will have distinctly different features from that of the Caribbean person, simply because of the variance in the experiences as persons being saved.

Clifford F. Payne, the first Caribbean theologian to articulate in writing some thoughts on Christ and ethnicity in the Caribbean, in his article "What Will A Caribbean Christ Look Like?" saw it as an inevitable question given the intensity of the search for Caribbean identity which existed in the 1970's. The questions he raised, I think, still remain very pertinent to us today. They are questions which address the credibility of the Caribbean person's belief in the incarnational reality of the Christ Event. He asked, "If Christ cannot be Caribbean, then can he speak to the deepest needs of Caribbean people? …. How do you deliver a people from the evil that is both within them and around them without becoming one like them in such a profound way that your identification with them is complete? That is not possible."[30] he says. This implies that, as people grow in deeper awareness of themselves - their gifts, their beauty and confidence of being loved - their God begins to take greater resemblance of persons within their immediate experience. If this does not happen, it means that God and Christ remain alien to them. For it is within our human experience that we can see ourselves as being saved, forgiven, healed, fathered, mothered, brothered, and sistered. Noel Erskins shows it to be a theological/christological imperative when he states that:

> Every race of people since time began who have attempted to describe their God by words, or by painting, or by carving, and form or figure, have conveyed the idea that the God who made and shaped their destinies was symbolised in themselves. [31]

The historical Jesus came to the people of Israel as they were a people in need of a saviour. He came among them as "the oppressed one" (as one of them) who was to save his people from their oppression. Therefore, the poor and the oppressed of his time were able to identify

---

[30] Clifford Payne, *Troubling of the Waters*, 1.

[31] Noel L. Erskins, *Decolonizing Theology: A Caribbean Perspective*, (Maryknoll, N.Y., Orbis Books, 1981, 88.

with him. From this principle, therefore, it is inevitable that Caribbean people, as a people in need of salvation, will see themselves in the Jesus of history. He is the one in whom God is incarnate and in whom every people and all peoples are called to partake and find their meaning. The task of Christianity, therefore, is to continue God's incarnation in Jesus by becoming contextual.

This is not a process of making Christ whom we want him to be. We simply recognise who he is for us within our historical experience. The New Testament tells us (as indicated above) that a certain kind of people were his particular friends, and so it is such people, from a subjective point of view, that determines the meaning and scope of Jesus Christ. The very name Jesus means Saviour, "*for God was in Christ reconciling the world to himself*" (2 Cor 5:19). But real salvation is always from within and not from without. Ontologically he becomes like all those destined to be saved because he becomes one of them in their historical reality. Speaking on behalf of the black community in the United States, James Cone expresses the truth of this reality. He states:

> The Christological importance of Jesus must be found in his blackness. If he is not black, then the resurrection has little significance to our time. If he cannot be what we are, we cannot be what he is. Our being with him is dependent on his being with us in

the oppressed black condition, revealing to us what is necessary for our liberation. [32]

What Cone spells out here is not far from the thoughts of the second-century Irenaeus who affirmed that "we could not otherwise have received eternity and immortality ... unless the Eternal and the Immortal One had first become what we are."[33] However Cone's use of blackness here is not limited to skin pigmentation, but rather it emphasises the reality of the experience of a people in a particular historical context - the context of oppression. Such was the experience of being Black in the United States. What then does this mean to us in the Caribbean?

Christ and Ethnicity in the Caribbean

To talk about Christology and ethnicity in the Caribbean can be a difficult subject given its multi-racial composition and the consequent mixtures that have resulted. More often than not the Caribbean person would speak in terms of the degree of the mixtures

---

[32] James Cone, *Liberation: A Black Theology of Liberation*, J.B. Cuppinutt Company, Philadelphia & New York, 1970, 212.

[33] Jacques Dupuis, S.J, *Who Do You Say I Am?: Introduction to Christology*, Orbis Books, Maryknoll, New York, 1994, 78 quoting Irenaeus, Adv. Haer., III,19,1; Sources chretiennes 34, 332.

which make up his/her ethnic reality. However, since our subject matter here is not limited to skin pigmentation or hair texture, we need to articulate what the quest of the Caribbean person is in that regard. The primary task at hand, I think, is to focus on what we refer to as the Caribbean experience; that which makes Caribbean people what they are. This calls for a consideration of the individual contributions of each component part and the people as a whole, to that Caribbean reality. This includes the contribution of the Blacks, East Indians, Javanese, Chinese, and also the Europeans. Payne had pointed out that the Christ of the Caribbean person "will become progressively black"[34] given the racial composition of the Caribbean, and he "will owe something to India."[35] He also felt that Christ will "still have European features,"[36] given the contents of the total Caribbean experience. Where are we in relation to this observation, and how far can we go with such christological speculations?

The development of Christology vis-a-vis ethnicity in the Caribbean, I think, has been a gradual one; and rightly so. It has evolved parallel to the theological strides which have happened within the consciousness of the Caribbean

---

[34] Clifford Payne, Troubling of the Waters, 5.

[35] Ibid., 6

[36] Ibid., 2

people. To clarify this point I wish to borrow Robert Schreiter's models which he uses to describe evolving local theologies in his book entitled *Constructing Local Theologies*. In this he articulates a process of development which occurs as a people grow into greater maturity and self-awareness. Though he deals specifically with the evolution of local theologies, I think it can be applied also to the process of Christological realisation of a people.

Schreiter recognises a three step movement in local churches seeking to articulate for themselves the meaning of their existence. He speaks first of a *translation stage (model)* of theological awareness. At this stage, as the name suggests, the belief systems of one culture are translated into another without much consideration for the culture itself. The form of evangelisation which corresponds to this stage is one whereby the experience of the mother Church seeks parallel manifestations into the new culture. Therefore the Christ of such a model will have all the features of the one perceived to be the evangelising Church. For the Caribbean, therefore, its Christ of necessity would have northern features. At best the value of this model is in its being just a first stage of Christological development.

The second stage is one of *adaptation*. In this model, the local culture begins to be taken more seriously. It seeks to understand the people's worldview, their context, values, customs and beliefs, but still tends to "force cultural data into foreign categories."[37] We may have found parallels to this stage of development in the Caribbean within the experience of the 1970s. It was a period of experimentation which followed the Second Vatican Council. Such was, one might say, the theological posture of that period. Though it sought to take the cultural forms of the Caribbean people more seriously, little changes took place in the minds of the majority. In St. Lucia, for example, attempts were made at creating a new consciousness by the use of paintings which depicted 'Christ as Black.' Three such murals were painted in different churches on the island. Initially, it was resisted by the local people, most of whom were themselves black. The same can be said of the use of folk music in the churches in all the Caribbean islands. However, even when they had come to the level of acceptance there was little movement from the conceptual trappings of the north. Christological images, therefore,

---

[37] Robert J. Schreiter, *Constructing Local Theologies*, Obris Books, Maryknoll, New York, 1986, 10.

were being forced into foreign categories. This second stage, however, is a more mature stage of development.[38]

The third stage of theological consciousness is that of contextualisation. This model evidently focuses directly on the cultural context of the life of the people in which their belief receives expression. It recognises the goodness found in them, focuses on their needs, and uses their historical context as the point of departure for theological reflection. At this level one will realise the inseparable

---

[38] Schreiter makes reference to the address of Pope Paul VI to the African Bishop in Kampala, Uganda in 1969 as representing the translation approach: "The expression, that is, the language and mode of manifesting this one Faith, may be manifold; hence, it may be original, suited to the tongue, the style, the genius, and the culture, of the one who professes this one Faith. From this point of view a certain parallelism is not legitimate, but desirable. An adaptation of the Christian life in the fields of pastoral, ritual didactic and spiritual activities is not only possible; it is even favored by the Church. The liturgical renewal is a living example of this. And in this sense you may, and you must, have an African Christianity. Indeed, you possess human values and characteristic forms of culture which can rise up to perfection such as to find in Christianity, a true superior fullness, and prove to be capable of a richness of expression all its own, and genuinely African. This may take time. It will require that your African souls become imbued to its depths with the secret charisms of Christianity, so that these charisms may then overflow freely, in beauty and wisdom, in the true African manner." Ibid., 11.

relationship between ethnicity and Christology. This "ethnographic approach," as Schreiter calls it, is by nature incarnational and deals directly with the question of identity. Therefore, to the question: "Is Jesus really Caribbean?" the answer is a resounding "Yes." Pope John Paul II alluded to this incarnational reality when he said to his Nairobi audience in 1980 that "in you Christ has himself become African."[39] Again the *Second Vatican Council Documents*, in its "Pastoral Constitution on the Church in the Modern World:" *Gaudium et Spes* affirms that "by His Incarnation, the Son of God, has in a certain way united himself with each man … He has truly been made one of us, like to us in all things except sin."[40] This being so, therefore, the Caribbean person begins to look within for liberation (salvation). There becomes less and less need to look outside for what is already within. In other words, this 'self-affirmation' helps to confirm the words of Jesus that "the Kingdom of Heaven is 'among' you" (Lk 17:21). This however, should not be mistaken as a need to become enclosed onto oneself at the exclusion of other peoples. In fact, there is need for shared experiences with other peoples and cultures. What it affirms is the fact that every person and all people are called to one salvation,

---

[39] Shorter, 1988, 61-62.

[40] Austin Flannery, O.P. (ed), "Pastoral Constitution of the Church in the Modern World" *Vatican Council II*, 923.

but which is only realised when they discover meaning in the person of the incarnated Jesus - the Jesus who became particular despite having a universal mission. In fact this universal mission had to be realised by coming through and to a particular people. This means that the choice of Israel in God's salvific plan was for this one reason - that by becoming particular in them, his Word would reach the ends of the earth. In this case, therefore, particularity comes before universality. That process continues today.

However, we are still left with the question as to what specific face Jesus would have. The particular configuration of such a face, I think, is in the minds, or more precisely, the collective consciousness of the Caribbean people. It is a face that would truly represent the people in their need for liberation. Practically, it is only symbolic. It is the face which represents Caribbean unity, Caribbean 'pride,' and finds value in sacrifice for the freedom of Caribbean people. A face which would symbolise any form of oppression or domination would be rejected. As holds true for all people, whenever true freedom is discovered in the person of Christ, every other image is rejected. The acceptance of the Christ image, therefore, is determined by its capacity to liberate and save.

Why a Caribbean Christology?

The first and basic reason why it is important to conceive a Caribbean Christology is because the theological endeavour today must address the reality of a people's life situation. It is not to remain only as an intellectual exercise. A genuine theology is really a reflection on the "God-experiences" in the lives of a people. In this way it is able to remain vital and relevant. Genuine theology is by a living people, about a living people and for a living people. However, theology also has the task of challenging the historical contexts of people in order to lead them to greater freedom. It has to be a vital agent in the transformation of faith into a culture, so to speak. When Pope John Paul II said that "a faith which does not become culture has not been fully lived out,"[41] he made direct reference to this fact. The work of the theologian, therefore can, (and ought) to challenge this into being - to bring about a Caribbean Christian civilisation.[42]

The second reason is because Christology determines pastoral action. A people's perception of Christ determines the content and method of their evangelisation and mission. It has a direct relationship with this mode of being Church (ecclesiology). A Christ who remains

---

[41] The Foundational Letters of the Pontifical Council on Culture, 1982.

[42] See Part 3.

foreign in the consciousness of a people reinforces poor self-worth. He leaves them with a kind of dependency syndrome which never liberates. The Christ from within, therefore, energises a people with self-love, which is vital for the realisation and acceptance of the love of God. A people who always have the need to look to someone else for salvation never learn to love and appreciate self. On the other hand, a people who believe in a Christ who identifies completely with them and has become one of them seek to build a Church which has the empowerment of each person and all its members as a primary pastoral policy. It addresses directly the situation of poverty on all levels; be they material, intellectual, social or religious. The maturity of a people is always reflected in its growth in "localness." This is where the incarnation finds its meaning. Working towards this end is an act of faith and an act of love. Our Christology therefore has to be incarnated, it has to be contextual; it has to be Caribbean.

Caribbean Theological Conference, Trinidad, June 1996

PART III

Towards A Caribbean Christian Civilization

Introduction

The primary agenda of the Christian Gospel is to lead persons to their fullest selves as human beings on the pattern of Jesus Christ, the model of ultimate human fulfillment.[43] It is a liberation process. Therefore the Christianization of a people can be described as a process of liberating them into being. In the Caribbean, it seems impossible to speak of a Christian civilization without first examining the historical development of the people vis-à-vis their experience of liberation through the Christian message. This third part will focus firstly on the Caribbean experience from a historical, socio-cultural and religious perspective. Secondly, it will look at some of the issues within that experience and the Christian responses that they suggest. Thirdly, it will look at some of the challenges that the future poses if it is to maintain a Christian posture.

History of the Caribbean

Much of who we are today as a people have been shaped by our history and the most prominent mark of Caribbean history is its colonial past. It has to do with the European involvement in the region from the latter part of the fifteenth century to the early part of

---

[43] Cf. General Directory for Catechesis, No.80, CCC, 4-6.

the twentieth century. It was practically five hundred years of exploration, exploitation and colonization of the New World by the Spanish, British, French and Dutch explorers. This history, according to Gordon K. Lewis, may be divided into three periods: (1) "The post-discovery period, covering the sixteenth, seventeenth and eighteenth centuries; (2) the post-emancipation period, that is, the period following the abolition of slavery (1833 in the British colonies, 1848 in the French colonies, 1863 in the Dutch colonies, 1873 in Puerto Rico, and 1886 in Cuba; and (3) the post-independence period.[44] They are coloured by incidents of rivalry between the four European colonizing nations for power and supremacy in the region and in Europe itself.

The earliest attempt at colonization and the quest for riches and power left the indigenous Amerindian population near extinction due to their exposure to unaccustomed working conditions and diseases. This subsequently gave rise to the African slave trade, as the demand for a strong labour force become increasingly necessary to support the growing agricultural economy. Within the period 1492-1870, Philip Curtin estimated

---

[44] Gordon K. Lewis., "The Contemporary Caribbean: A General Overview," in Sydney W. Mintz and Sally Price, eds. *Caribbean Contours*, Baltimore, John Hopkins University Press, 1985, 222.

that a total of 9,566,000 African slaves were imported into the Americas.[45]

The plantation became the main social institution known to the African slaves, and it formed an integral part of the social structure in which the planter (owning) class was on top and the black (slave/non-owning) class was at the bottom and "the brown mulatto group (the so-called people of colour or free coloureds) in between."[46]

The abolition of slavery had far reaching social consequences as the slaves abandoned the sugar plantations. Many moved to the hills to settle as peasants, while others moved to the towns seeking employment and new trades.[47] Only a few remained on the plantations, thus giving rise to a labour problem for the planters. At first a few European immigrants came to work on limited contracts, but this proved unsuccessful. Then the attention was turned towards the East. According to Mintz's estimates, "over 135,000 Chinese, nearly half a million Indians and more than 33,000 Javanese reached

---

[45] Philip D. Curtin, *The Atlantic Slave Trade: A Census*, Madison, University of Wisconsin Press, 1969, 268

[46] Lewis, op.cit. 222.

[47] Cf. F. R. Augier & S. C. Gordon, *Making of the West Indies*, Longman Caribbean Ltd., London, 1979, 165-167.

the Caribbean."[48] A small number of Jews, Lebanese, Irish and Syrians were recorded.[49]

The Haitian revolution of 1803 inaugurated the independence era in the Caribbean. "Cuba and the Dominican Republic were nominally independent, but in fact were under United States domination for much of the twentieth century."[50] The former British territories[51] and the former Dutch territories of Surinam gained the political independence in the twentieth century. There are four sets of territories still under colonial or quazi-colonial arrangements, "(1) The British Virgin Islands and Bermuda, (2) the Dutch Islands of the Netherlands Antilles (Aruba, Bonaire and Curacao), (3) Puerto Rico and the U.S. Virgin Islands, (4) the French departments of Martinique,

---

[48] Sidney W. Mintz, *Caribbean Transformations*, Baltimore, John Hopkins University Press, 1974, 313.

[49] Cf. F. R. Augier & S. C. Gordon, *The Making of the West Indies*, Longman Caribbean Ltd., London, 1979, 195-210; Tony Martin, *Caribbean History: From Pre-Colonial Origins to the Present,* Pearson Education, Inc., New York, 2012, 211-247.

[50] Michael M. Horowitz, ed., *People and Cultures in the Caribbean*, New York, National History Press, 1971, 3.

[51] The British territories were granted independence from Great Britain in the following order; Jamaica and Trinidad & Tobago, 1962; Guyana and Barbados, 1966; Dominica, 1978; St. Lucia and St. Vincent, 1979; Belize, 1981; Antigua, 1982; St. Kitts-Nevis, 1983.

Guadeloupe and French Guyana. St. Maarten is divided between the French and the Dutch, with the northern two-thirds of the island administered by Guadeloupe and the Southern third by the Netherlands Antilles."[52]

For the Caribbean states independence meant the ability to engage in political and economic and social dialogue with other nations and being accountable only to themselves. A significant part also entailed internal self-government with its local leadership. However, most of the Caribbean islands have retained the form of government as practiced in Europe.

The Church and Colonialism

A significant part of the history of the Caribbean has been shaped by the presence of the European Church. From the very start the Spanish pioneers exhibited a strong link between Altar and Throne in the expansion of Spanish rule in the New World. This was the time when, according to Idris Hamid, "there was no clear division between State and Church … The State was the Church and the Church was the State[53] in Europe. Therefore, "the Church in Spanish America was an overseas extension of

---

[52] Mintz, 1974, 313.

[53] Idris Hamid, *A History of the Presbyterian Church in Trinidad 1868-1968*, St. Andrew's Theological College, 1980, 12.

the Church in Spain and for a long time was a reflection of Spanish culture."[54]

The Church in Spanish America went along with the exploitation of the indigenous people even to the point of owning land and slaves. The cause of these oppressed natives was unsuccessfully protested by priests like Montesenos and Las Casas in the mid-sixteenth century.[55] With the coming of the British in the seventeenth century the Anglican Church became the official Church in some of the colonies. "Its relationship to the new territories and slaves was remarkably similar to the earlier relationship of the Spanish Church."[56] The introduction of the African slave trade as a source of cheap labour for the New World plantation societies was supported by the Church through the rationale that "firstly … the slaves were slaves in Africa already and secondly, that coming into a Christian society they would have the opportunity for conversion."[57] However, in becoming Christian the end didn't justify the means.

---

[54] John T. Harricharan, *The Catholic Church in Trinidad 1498-1852*, Trinidad: Inprint, 1972, 4.

[55] Cf. F. R. Augier & S. C. Gordon, *The Making of the West Indies*, Longman Caribbean Ltd., London, 1979, 21.

[56] Hamid, 1980, 25.

[57] F. R. Augier, &, S. Gordon., eds., *The Making of the West Indies*, Trinidad/Jamaica, Longman Caribbean Ltd. 1970, 137.

On the plantations, missionary activities were at first largely unsuccessful. The Catholic Church, for example, made little progress with the mass of slaves in the French colonies because of the unwavering opposition of the planters and many of the government officials in the islands. "The reason for this opposition was that planters feared the consequences of religious instructions for slaves, who might thereby get new ideas about their worth as humans and rebel against their servile conditions."[58] "Marriage among slaves was uncommon and was certainly not encouraged on the estates. Men and women changed partners without regard for permanent unions.[59] Some clergy shared the planters' views against the conversion of the slaves.

With the conversion of many ex-slaves and indentured workers to Christianity, the new Caribbean Church entered the independence era with a membership of varied cultural backgrounds. The Catholic and other mainline Protestant Churches, however, continued to reflect significantly the image of the European Church in its clergy, its missionary dynamic, its vision and its architecture.

---

[58] Ibid., 135.

[59] Ibid., 137.

Gabriel Malzaire

The Culture of the Caribbean

The Caribbean region's rich variety in ethnic and religious composition, its cultural and historical plurality, has helped to create and shape what was often referred to as a "Caribbean culture." Some writers have argued against a distinct culture for the Caribbean.[60] However, it cannot be denied that there are dominant features within the history of the people, such as the African slave trade and the plantation social system, which have produced common cultural features within the entire Caribbean community. The influence of East Indians, Europeans, Chinese, among others, have added their own flavour to the Caribbean world-view. Arguably, what we call a "Caribbean culture" is more a conglomeration of cultures rather than a single culture. The dominant cultural feature in each individual Caribbean island or mainland territory is dependent on their relative powers, that is, the size

---

[60] "It is inaccurate to refer to the Caribbean as a "cultural area" if by "culture" is meant a common body of historical tradition. The very diverse origins of Caribbean populations; the complicated history of European cultural impositions; and the absence in most societies of any firm continuity of the culture of the colonial power have resulted in a very heterogeneous cultural picture." Sidney W. Mintz, "The Caribbean as a Sub-cultural Area," *Peoples and Cultures of the Caribbean, An Anthropological Reader*, ed. Michael M. Horowitz, The Natural History Press, New York, 1971, 19-20

of the racial and ethnic grouping, language dominance, traditional customs and religious prominence.

Language is one of the primary medium for transmitting culture. The four official languages spoken in the Caribbean are English, French, Spanish and Dutch. In most parts there are one or more dialects spoken as a result of the cross-fertilization between the various languages, giving rise to the French Creole (Patois) and Papiamento (Dutch Creole). In most of the English speaking Caribbean, an English Creole has developed but they vary slightly from one island to another. Some Hindi is still spoken in Trinidad, Guyana and Jamaica by the East Indian descendants.

The use of Creole and non-standard forms in the Caribbean liturgies has been a slow development in the Caribbean. In the French-based Creole speaking islands like St. Lucia and Dominica, while the Creole was more readily accepted for preaching in the more rural parts, it was at first considered an 'insult' to urban hearing. However, the language of liturgical music (sacred music, as it is sometimes called), for a long time, reflected the spirit of the Roman Church with little or no local flavor. Trinidad too expressed discomfort with the use of the non-standard English in its Christian liturgies up to the late 1970. Martinique and Guadeloupe had their share of

Gabriel Malzaire

difficulties at attempts to "creolize" their liturgies. With the recent upsurge in the awareness of the importance of local cultural expressions in worship, there has been a greater innovation in the Caribbean Church's use of the people's language.

Race and Colour in the Caribbean

The racial situation in the Caribbean and its colour configurations has deep roots in the socio-economic and socio-political structures introduced during the days of colonization and slavery. First of all, the plantation society in the Caribbean was based on a system whereby the white owning class was at the top and the black African (non-owning) class was at the bottom of the social structure. Between those two extremes were the mulattos or coloured people (the offspring of white slave masters and female slaves). Skin colour determined one's position on the social ladder. There was an established gradation of skin colour. The lighter skin colour, of course, preferred to the darker one. However, this obsessive colour consciousness was partially altered after Emancipation. With the coming of the different ethnic groups into the Caribbean (e.g. Chinese, East Indians, Javanese, Syrian, Lebanese) the mode of social stratification became very inconsistent. A further shift began to happen when the ex-slaves and their descendants began to own land and enter the professional and business fields.

It is significant to note that the leaders of the Church up to the last forty years were foreign, mostly European. Even today a significant percentage of the clergy are expatriates; however, the configuration has shifted. In Saint Lucia and Dominica, for example, the shift has been towards continental Africa, the Philippines and India. In 2015 only 10.3% of the priests serving in St. Lucia were European while 50% were local Caribbean. The remaining 39.7% are from Africa, the Philippines and India. In Dominica 11.1% are European while 66.6% are local Caribbean.

Traditional Religion and Culture

While the Caribbean was "christianized" by 'Christian' Europe, the African slaves, East Indians immigrants and others, brought with them their individual religious belief systems and cultural practices. The Indian Hindu culture had its influence in Trinidad, Guyana and Jamaica. At the same time the African population because of its numerical strength, had untold influence in shaping the way of life in the Caribbean. The presence of the Shango cult in Trinidad, Pocomania in Jamaica, Vodun in Haiti and Obeah in many of the territories have their effects on the Caribbean world-view.

"The Rastafarian movement (cult) was started in Jamaica in 1930 soon after the coronation of Ras Tafari – Haile Selassie – as Emperor of Ethiopia. Haile Selassie believed himself to be the only true lineal descendant to King David and also the 225th of the line of Ethiopian kings stretching back to the Queen of Sheba."[61]

Rastafarians refer to God as JAH. "Their religious belief is interwoven with their cultural, political and economic life-style."[62] From the 1950s to 1970s the movement spread throughout the Caribbean particularly among the youth. For many, however, it was more a fashion than a religion. The Jamaican reggae music has been a main channel through which the philosophy has spread, especially in

---

[61] Kortright Davis, *Mission for Caribbean Change*, Frankfurt, Peter Lang, 1982, 110. In terms of spiritual significance, few dates compete with April 21, 1966, in the hearts of Rastafari. Celebrated by the faithful the world over as Coronation Day, it marks the visit to Jamaica by the Emperor of Ethiopia, Haile Selassie I, a figure worshipped as a deity by Rastafari everywhere. Selassie was born Tafari Makonnen Woldemikael on July 23, 1892, in the Ethiopian village of Ejersa Goro; "Ras" is a noble honorific—thus, Ras Tafari). Haile Selassie died in Aug. 1975, almost a year after he was deposed in a military coup. There is no consensus, among historians or among Rastasfari, on whether he died of medical complications while under house arrest in Addis Ababa, or was assassinated.

[62] Ibis., 111.

the 1970s with the advent of the reggae artist, Bob Marley. In spite of his death in 1981, he continues to live in the minds of millions through his music.

Most of the cults and religions mentioned above have African origins, but have been adapted to the new Caribbean setting. Although the Rastafarian movement (cult) is a Jamaican creation, it points to Ethiopia (the Promised Land) as the prime reason for its existence. All of the above, in one way or another, have their effects on the Christian Church (experience) in the Caribbean.

The Effect of History on the Caribbean as a People

A people with such a history as mentioned above can hardly escape being scarred and wounded in one way or another. Theirs was an experience of deracination followed by an experience of non-personhood through a process of negative reinforcements. Those scars went deeper than many Caribbean people themselves are ready to admit. It seems almost indelible, so much so that it has affected the people's way of seeing themselves and their way of being themselves. The task of the missionary to the Caribbean is not only to preach the Good News but to allow it to incarnate itself in a process of historical and cultural liberation. The question for us is, how far has it done so, and how much is it continuing to do so?

The question of poor self-esteem is pertinent to Caribbean people. Our history has taught us to see ourselves in relation to others; that is, how we approximate ourselves to them and their values. It is a system in which one's sense of worth has been determined by its proximity to the white and foreign. This has repercussions on all levels of the Caribbean reality: politics, economics, culture and religion. Everything from outside is better than what is home-grown. It works like a kind of psychological condition of compensation whereby one constantly looks outside of self for satisfaction to his/her inadequacy. Our perspective is a non-Caribbean perspective; thus the perpetuation of poverty, dependency and alienation remains a challenge.

The Theological Question

With such a perspective, God becomes foreign to us and it becomes very difficult to identify with him. The attempts at evangelization from the very early days of colonization were done from a northern perspective, but not from the perspective of the evangelized. Additionally, the God that was presented was a God with all northern features, but not a God who seems to have been able to incarnate Himself in the Caribbean reality. In his comments on that aspect of the Caribbean experience Idris Hamid sees that the understanding of the faith, the expression of its creeds, beliefs and particularly worship, suffers from an incongruity with the "every-day-ness" of our life. As such, the God presented to us is not seen as that one who relates to the Caribbean "every-day-ness," or as one who enters our everyday experience. He says, "What it boils down to is that we were trained to worship God through somebody else's experience."[63] He asserts further:

> In the religious imagination of our people he is a ... foreigner ... Even the categories of our religious experiences are imports which do not reflect our cultural and native experiences. We experience God as an outsider.[64]

The Christological Question

This theological situation or challenge naturally leads us to ask Christological questions. If one of the tasks of the evangelizing mission of the Church is to incarnate the Gospel of Christ, it follows therefore that this Christ whose brother and sister we become in our very being by our baptism will begin to take our features. As has been pointed out in Part II, an incarnational Christology

---

[63] Idris Hamid, "Theology and Caribbean Development," in David Mitchell, ed., With *Eyes Wide Open*, Bridgetown, Barbados: CADEC, 1973, 122.

[64] Ibid., 122

is really the basis for talking about a Caribbean Christ, to which our colonial legacy hardly gave any thought. The fact that God entered history in the person of Jesus, and through His life, death and resurrection, brought to humankind a unique possibility of experiencing life to the fullest is the Incarnation. This is central to Christian faith. Moreover, it was through the reflection of the disciples' historical experience of Jesus that they came to recognize him as the Christ and God-incarnate. It helps us to put into focus the significance of the life, mission, death and resurrection of the historical Jesus. From that stand-point, we can establish how Jesus can be the Christ of the Jew, the Black, and the White and by extension, the whole world.

Therefore the incarnational process which finds its climax in the person of Jesus Christ celebrates the fact that God enters fully and participates completely in the life of the people whom he desires to save. This process tells a great deal about God's manner of communicating with humanity in Jesus Christ. Such a profound entry into the human situation is known as identification. This no doubt gives a deeper understanding of the Genesis 1:27 affirmation of humanity being created in the image and likeness of God. It may be significant here to make mention of the apparition of our Blessed

Lady of Guadeloupe in 1531, though it is not directly a Christological issue. Tradition has it that she came in the form of a Mexican peasant, and I would well imagine she spoke the language of the peasant. In that instance, therefore, Our Lady became Mexican. In the same way Jesus becomes Caribbean in the Caribbean context.

It is important to note, however, that the use of ethnic language to describe the Jesus of the Caribbean person is not limited to colour configurations. It is rather meant to help us come to a deeper understanding of our own self-worth, which is a pre-requisite for real liberation and salvation. Inevitably, the Jesus of the Caribbean person is the Jesus of the Gospel who is saviour of all humankind.

The Ecclesiological Question

From our own experience of Christianity, we would understand that theology and Christology are empty without a context and the 'proper' context for these is the Church – the *ekklesia.* It is in the Church that these concepts are fleshed and lived out.

We have already noted above that in colonial times the Church in the Caribbean was an extension of the Church in Europe in all its shapes and forms. The theology was a top-descending one rather than a bottom-ascending one.

Its priesthood obviously was schooled in that mind-set, and therefore the experience of Church was of little difference. It lacked a proper incarnational dimension, one might say. The ecclesiology of the Caribbean Church was measured according to its proximity to the way of being Church as perceived in the north. This determined the form of worship and liturgy, and the mode of evangelization. But conscious of that lack, Vatican Council II throws light on the primary focus of missionary activity when it says:

> In order to bear witness to Christ, fruitfully, they (missionaries) should establish relationships of respect and love with those men, they should acknowledge themselves as members of the group in which they live, and through the various undertakings and affairs of human life they should share in their social and cultural life. They should be familiar with the national and religious traditions and uncover with gladness and respect those seeds of the Word which lie hidden among them.[65]

In another place the document reiterated:

> Whoever is to go among another people must hold their inheritance, language and way of life in great esteem.[66]

---

[65] Austin P. Flannery, ed., *Vatican Council II*, "Decree on the Church's Missionary Activity: Ad Gentes, 1965, No. 11.

[66] Ibid., No. 26.

Historically, we never seemed to have been able to produce a form good enough to approximate the foreign ones. As Hamid rightly points out, "Man and his cultural historical milieu are not two separate realities. Rather, man is part and parcel of the cultural historical milieu; so that, rejection of the latter inescapably involves rejection of man himself. In other words, you cannot throw cold water on a man's cultural-historical life without giving him the chills. Or, if you prefer, you can't chop up a man's cultural-historical setting (milieu) without causing injury to the man."[67] Commenting on the liturgy, he adds:

> God had to be communicated in a language which is not ours. It led to a loss of faith in our elements – our milieu ... Ours was never good enough for him to enter to meet us. God was made to stand outside that milieu, not because he is that kind of God, but because he was trapped in liturgy.[68]

This is by no means a critique of the function of liturgy *per se*. The celebration of liturgy has, of necessity, to reflect the experience and manner of being of the people as they relate to God. Liturgy ought to be celebrated in such a way that people express their true selves. Caribbean people are a people of rhythm and tempo – a swinging people. Music naturally resonates in the gut of the Caribbean person.

---

[67] Hamid, 1973, 128.

[68] Ibid., 128.

We must admit that in recent years, with the improved awareness of the importance of local cultural expressions in worship, there have been greater innovations in the Caribbean Church's use of cultural forms which are closer to the Caribbean expression. Obviously there is still room for improvement.

The Challenge of Traditional Religions

In the midst of all the celebration of the high Church liturgies, there is still among the members of Churches in the Caribbean an influence of the traditional religions (cults) practices. The above-mentioned are Vodun in Haiti, Shango in Trinidad, Pocomania in Jamaica, Santeria in Cuba and Obeah in many of the territories. They no doubt pose a challenge to authentic Christianity. The basic question is one of divided loyalty to the deity. Commenting on the Haitian situation, George E. Simpson says that "a majority of vodunists are Catholics, but most of these people do not seem very sincere in their Catholicism. The old traditions persist, the African gods are still real to them, and they cannot rely on the Church ... There is no difficulty in being both Catholic and the servant of the loas."[69] This is especially so "since members of the vodun cult believe that saints are the loas, although they hold that not all are saints."[70]

In Cuba the worship of the African deities is known as Santaria. Bascom asserts that:

> Santaria is a vital, growing institution, practiced throughout the entire length of the island, in both rural and urban areas; in the latter, in fact, it is probably the strongest. In recent years it seems to have been expanding, recruiting additional members from the Negro, the mixed and even the white population.[71]

He speaks of some features of the Santeria, which include, "the syncretism of African deities with Catholic saints commonly represented by colourful pictures; the African pattern of possession which has attracted interest

---

[69] George E. Simpson, "The Belief Systems of Haitian Vodun" in Peoples and Cultures in the Caribbean, Op. cit., 504. By far the most prominent feature in the Vodun cult's realm of the sacred are the 'loas'. Many of the 'loas' are African deities who have been inherited through succeeding generations by the descendants of those who brought them to Haiti. Both Herkovits and Courlander reports that some of the 'loas' are indigenous to Haiti, and they agree that these 'loas' are the result of the deification of powerful ancestors, 494-495.

[70] Ibid., 495.

[71] William Bascom, "The Focus of Cuban Santeria," *Peoples and Cultures of the Caribbean*, 522.

as a psychological phenomenon, and the retention of animal sacrifices and African drumming, singing and dancing in the New World Negro rituals."[72]

In some islands, the regular visit of some Church members to the village seer or fortune teller is prominent. His/her job is to read the lives of the client to prescribe remedies for a cure, or the course of action to be taken to prevent the predictable misfortunes. The obeah woman/man was visited to put harmful spells on the enemies of their clients. This practice has been prevalent since the period of slavery. Augier and Gordon tell us:

> The slaves had their own ritual beliefs which had nothing to do with Christianity. Obeah-men were sometimes detected on the estates … some obeah-men hid in the bush and lived on the offerings brought by clients. Some planters believed that they frightened their victims to death, or even poisoned them if this failed.[73]

While the practice may be significantly less in the Caribbean today, it no doubt added a superstitious slant to the people's beliefs.

The Rastafarian movement (cult), as we have mentioned, appeals to the need of the lower class and

---

[72] Ibid., 522

[73] Augier and Gordon, 1970. 136.

the youth "who would be completely out of place in the orthodox Churches."[74] They serve as a reactionary group who express their dissatisfaction with western society and its values by their life-style. Though much of the philosophy has created a fashion rather than a religion for many, the influence has been of a significant consequence. Dissatisfied youth and victims of oppressive situations and conditions find an easy recourse in the movement by adopting the hair-style, the jargon, and décor, i.e. wearing the iets (red), green and gold colours in their outfits, and proud to be referred to as "dread." Others have little allegiance to the philosophy but capitalize on the drug trade that it engenders. However, those who are faithful to the philosophy pursue a life of peaceful union with nature free from the sophistication of the Western society.

Given the foregoing, could it be that the persistence of these religions groups was due to the way evangelization was done? It may have overlooked the religious psychology of the people and instead of using elements of those religions and purifying them of superstitions, as was done in the Roman Empire in early Christianity; instead it simply disregarded them as "evil." The Rastafarian movement, can be viewed be as a radical reaction to a

---

[74] Davis, 1982, 111.

Christianity that may have disregarded the incarnational principle.

The Moral Question

Ethics has often been described as the cutting edge of theology. It focuses on morality and human behaviour. It is virtually impossible to talk of a Christian civilization without raising the issues that impinge on our moral decisions. I will open this discussion with a statement by Archbishop Fulton J. Sheen of revered memory. In one of his speeches to a priest retreat towards the end of his life, he said:

> I believe that we are now living at the end of Christendom; the end of Christendom, not the end of Christianity. What is Christendom? Christendom is the political, economic, moral, social, legal life of a nation as inspired by the Gospel ethic. This is finished. Abortion, breakdown of family life, dishonesty, even the natural virtues upon which the supernatural virtues were based are being discredited. Christianity is not at the end; but we are at the end of Christendom. And the sooner we face up to this fact, the sooner we will be able to solve our many problems … We will have to begin to be a different Church … We are between the death of an old civilization and culture and the swing to the beginning of a new. The old is

dead and powerless, and the new is powerless to be born. These are the times in which we live.[75]

Archbishop Sheen is here presenting a universal situation. He raises all the main issues that pertain to the moral question today: politics, economics, social communication and values, the law and moral behaviour. All these are very broad issues, but for our purposes, we will limit our discussions to the challenge that they pose to the Caribbean Church for an appropriate Christian response.

Politics

The politics of the Caribbean, as can be deduced from earlier findings, evolved out of a colonial experience of domination and dependence. The so called 'Independence era' began with Haiti since 1803 through the revolutionary method, and since then many of the other Caribbean islands and mainland territories have experienced various degrees of self-government, especially in the latter half of the twentieth century. These were supposedly efforts to bring about change that would confront the existing structures of the political system in such a way as would enable the people in the region to participate more effectively and with greater self-confidence in charting

---

[75] Fulton J. Sheenn (Archbishop), Talk at a retreat fro priests.

their own course for the future. However, the political history of Haiti until this present age; the experience of Grenada with its socialist presence from 1979 to 1983, the political machinery that existed in Guyana under the Burnham regime and its consequent economic slump, has left much to be desired. The inadequacies of the political machinery that we can raise in speaking about the various Caribbean countries will be just a matter of degree.

In the light of this, the Church has a moral responsibility. It "can be neither aloof nor silent, for in so doing it will sin,"[76] says Hamid. He stresses that, while it may not be true to say that the Caribbean Churches were not involved in politics, "many gave powerful support even through their silence to the political issues of the day."[77] In his opinion, we cannot but be involved, if the principle that guides the action of the Church remains the love for the human person. Working for the common good will necessarily keep the Church alert to unjust political acts. Such positions are very precarious, conflicting and subject to much compromise. In situations where Church leaders have attempted to address pertinent political questions which affect the lives of the people, politicians are known to have said, "Let us fill the bellies of the people and you

---

[76] Idris Hamid, 1973, 131.

[77] Ibid., 131.

take care of their souls."[78] In a climate of such dichotomy between politics and religion, good Christians often leave the political arena to those who are power seeking, and who have little concern for the people but are in pursuit of personal benefits.

At the third General Conference of Latin American Bishops in Puebla in 1979 it was affirmed that "the Church feels it has a duty and a right to be present in this area of reality; for Christianity is supposed to evangelize the whole of human life, including the political dimension. So the Church criticizes those who would restrict the scope of faith to personal or family life; those who would exclude the professional, economic, social and political order as if sin, love, prayer and pardon had no relevance in them."[79] The Church ought to stand as an avant-garde to the political machinery. It "helps to foster the values that should inspire politics … interpreting the aspirations of the people, especially the yearnings of those that society tends to marginalize."[80] Consequently, the questions of poverty, unemployment, and injustice will not be handled superficially, but she will study their causes and the means of eliminating them.

---

[78] Statement by a St. Lucian politician.

[79] Third General Conference of Bishops of Latin America, *Puebla*, 1979, 109.

[80] Ibid., 110.

Gabriel Malzaire

The Economy

Economics and politics can hardly be separated because a country's economy has much to do with political decision-making. We have seen that the human condition has been directly affected by the socio-economic and political condition, and that the dialectic of domination and dependence continues to be at the center of the Caribbean experience. Davis is of the opinion that "the way forward requires radical changes that will confront the existing structures of the economic system in such a way as would enable all the people in the region to participate more effectively and with greater self-confidence and deeper meaning in the total process."[81] He goes on to say that "the demand for economic liberation rests very heavily on the need for a radical change in the political will of the region, such as would enable the poor majority to share in the public apparatus of decision-making."[82]This seems especially appropriate in the present era. There is a greater need for creativity in using all the local available resources intelligently to produce a viable economy. The apparatus has of necessity to be home grown. The more we look outside of ourselves for solutions, the more alienated we become as a people. This is not withstanding the

[81] Davis, 1982, 179.

[82] Ibid., 179.

obvious interdependence that exists between and among
the nations of the world. It is obvious that the economics
of the world are interconnected. The price of oil on the
world market, for example, affects the Trinidad economy;
the rate of the British pound affects the price of bananas
in the Windward Islands; a glut of raw materials on an
international market will inevitably affect the price of
exports; and the list goes on. I am here referring to a need
for a re-examination of the value systems which will set
the priorities for economic development; one which will
cause us to be measured by our own standards rather
than that of others. We cannot afford to move like the
multi-national when we are not. Here the warning of Pope
Francis holds true when he calls the world to *say no to a
financial system which rules rather than serves.*[83]

The Church therefore has to be supportive of
such initiatives and even provide inspiration for self-
determination that would bring about genuine liberation
in the lives of a Caribbean people. Many great efforts have
been made in the area of the Credit Union movement, but
we need to look further at greater attempts towards self-
sufficiency in areas of agriculture and livestock to feed our
people, and small industries to meet the needs of the region.

---

[83] Pope Francis, Apostolic Exhortation: *Evangelii Gaudium* (The
Joy of the Gospel), Vatican Press, Rome, Nov. 24, 2013, No. 57.

Justice

The Post Vatican II Document entitled "*Justice in the World*" sets the stage for the discussion on the Church's mission to justice in the world when it says:

> Action on behalf of justice and participation in the transformation of the world fully appears to us as a constitutive dimension of the preaching of the Gospel, or, in other words, of the Church's mission for the redemption of the human race and its liberation from every oppressive situation.[84]

This mandate calls for an in-depth understanding of the virtue of charity. We cannot be satisfied with the giving of handouts as the major Christian response to the alleviation of human problems and human needs. Our vision cannot be limited to the problems only, but should concern ourselves with the "why" and the "how" of the situation as it pertains to the liberation of those in need. The exercise of justice has far-reaching implications and can happen on many levels: (i) on the level of employment situations and conditions – wages and salaries; (ii) on the level of racial and gender discrimination; (iii) on the level of human rights; and (iv) on the level of the cause of the poor and marginalized. However, as we become more

---

[84] Austin Flannery, O.P. ed. "Justice in the World," *Vatican Council II*, Vol. 2, 1971, 696.

alert to the constitutive segment of our mission we must be perceived as truly working to eradicate it within our own institutions and in our varied apostolates. We must not give double messages lest we lose credibility.

In the Pastoral Letter of the Antilles Episcopal Conference of 1975 entitled Justice and Peace in a New Caribbean, the Bishops openly confessed to the Church's guilt in its participation and perpetuation of unjust situations in the Caribbean. It reads as follows:

> We want to confess here, in all frankness and humility, that the record of our Church in this respect has not always been as good as it should have been. In spite of the example of many dedicated priests and religious who have lived among the poor and fully shared in their hardships, too often the Church we represent has seemed to be on the side of the wealthy and powerful. And in order to maintain a position of privilege, it has sometimes closed its eyes to wrongs and injustice crying out for redress. The long colonial past of the Church sometimes acted as if it were part of the establishment, condoning either openly or by its silence the existing order. And in the post-colonial era the Church in some places has not accepted the need for change with sufficient alacrity and good will. Our Church has also been guilty on occasion of acts of racial discrimination and of perpetuating social and class divisions.[85]

---

[85] Pastoral Letter of the Antilles Bishops' Conference, *Justice and Peace in a New Caribbean*, 1975, 6.

This humble disposition is one that the Church in the Caribbean needs to retain in order to be effective in ministering the Gospel in truth and sincerity. The poor has to be priority in all our pastoral planning because they were a priority for Jesus in his ministry. He got involved in their lives not in a superficial way, but in a personal and self-sacrificing way. We are called to do the same. This is our challenge.

Social Values

Any group of people who depend on others to define who they are has an acute problem of self-esteem, and consequently, a problem with their value system. In the Caribbean we have an inside knowledge of that reality. The Christian task in that regard is to be vigilant to the unwanted values that are creeping into today's society and to present a message that will challenge Caribbean people to be different. It is a message which will teach people to find beauty and dignity in themselves; one which will teach the truth that we don't have to be big to be of consequence. It will call for a vision of economic and social development in which people matter – and that is, all the people. Not an adoption of the 'survival of the fittest' ethic. William Demas, a prophet of the Caribbean economic world, gave some vital insights to genuine economic development in the region, which, I am sure, can be applied by the Church in her outlook. He said:

> The critical area in which change is required is in that of values. Only a change of values would hold hope for a solution to the unemployment problem ... Only a change of values would enable the people to accept a revised definition of development itself and reject the Madison Avenue definition of the "Good life." Only a change of values could contain the revolution of rising expectations for material improvement. Only a change of values could give the people the motivation to build from below.[86]

This change necessarily calls for a calculated fight against the view that materialism and individualism are philosophies for the development of a Caribbean people. It is a fight against the quick-success mentality which is rapidly grabbing the young Caribbean mind. The soap opera mentality of fashions and expedience is also posing a threat.

There is a constant challenge for the Church to be consistent in its value judgment and judgment of human

---

[86] William Demas, *The Political Economy of the English-speaking Caribbean, Barbados,* CADEC, 31; Roy G. Neehall, *With Eyes Wide Open,* "Christian Witness and Mission in Caribbean Development," 23.

behaviour. Hamid points out some of those possible imbalances when he said:

> Nudity in films is promptly condemned, but violence in the same film goes virtually unnoticed. We are still quick to condemn chicken stealing, but silent on the theft of human labour and substance. We condemn drunkenness among the lower classes but remain silent over the wasteful self-indulgence of the rich. We condemn the overt violence, especially those committed by the lower or non-income groups, but say little against the system of violence administered by the higher income groups under which people labour and live, and fraternize with some who perpetuate social injustice. We allow our priests and ministers the freedom to attend a cocktail party, but feel uneasy when they stand in solidarity with a group of workmen seeking economic justice and social redress.[87]

These are important considerations which call to bear on our integrity as Church. Only the constant task of vision-clarification for ministry and for the Church's presence can adequately deal with such questions. This is the task of the Caribbean Church.

Sexual Morality

The area of human sexuality has retained a controversial position whenever presented as an ethical

---

[87] Hamid, 1973. 132.

issue. However, it cannot be overlooked, especially since it has direct relation to the human family.

The family, as we know it, is the primary institution for socializing persons into their own sexuality. It is there that family members discover their maleness and femaleness, and their ability to interact as social beings. The ethicist John L. Thomas tells us:

> Considered from the viewpoint of the individual, sex appears both as a way of being and relating to the world, and a way of being in relation to others... Considered from the viewpoint of society, it appears as the basis of that primary human community of life and love, variously designed to provide for the mutual development and happiness of the couple, the orderly fulfillment of their sexually associated needs, and the adequate recruitment of new members of society through responsible personhood.[88]

As a moral issue, sexuality has often been presented negatively; hence the apparent inability of many persons to approach it with a healthy honesty. In order to instill a wholesome understanding of sex in our society, we need to remove many of the misconceptions that surround it, and consider it for what is really is. This inclination to

---

[88] John L. Thomas, S.J., "The Catholic Tradition for Responsibility in Sexual Ethics," in John C. Wynn, ed., *Sexual Ethics and Christian Responsibility*, New York, Association Press, 1970, 119.

regard everything related to sex as somehow stained with moral evil, has caused great discomfort among parents in providing adequate guidance for a more positive Christian attitude towards sexuality. True Christian ethics embraces the fact that the physical is not intrinsically evil, even if it can be used for that purpose. The same would be true of sexual desires and activity. In themselves, they are of no moral value; therefore, it is the conscious decision to use them against the right order that makes them sinful.

It must be understood that sexual behaviour is culturally based. In that regard, all known human societies from the beginning, have developed norms which determine appropriate expressions of sex among their members. With the conglomeration of cultural patterns in the Caribbean, there is no doubt that the understanding of sexual behaviour will be different and sometimes conflicting. The tension for us might be between the Western Christian understanding and African/East Indian perception.

Thomas points out that "in general, a review on relevant cross-cultural data indicates that past societies have followed two fairly well defined, though not mutually exclusive, approaches in formulating their system of sexual control."[89] They are the "society-centered"[90] system and the "person-centered"[91] system. According to him:

> Most cultures developed outside the Jewish and Christian spheres of influence have followed this society-centered approach in developing their sexual code. Since the general welfare, rather than sex itself, is the major focus of concern, these codes are designed either to ensure social order, or to secure divine protection ... Sexual conduct becomes the object of moral concern only to the extent that it relates to group interest ... The person-centered approach focuses concern on the individual and his personal responsibility for all voluntary, conscious use of his sexual faculties ... The use of sex in this personalist approach is evaluated primarily in terms of the perfection of the person, and in practice, sexual controls will appear to focus on the sexual faculty itself, rather than on those specific expressions of sex that the group may judge to be particularly disruptive of social order. This means that the deliberate, conscious use of sex will be regarded as morally good, to the extent that it conforms to what is believed to constitute the fulfillment of the person's divinely designed nature and destiny.[92]

---

[89] Ibid., 122.

[90] Ibid., 122.

[91] Ibid., 122.

[92] Ibid., 122-123.

How do those two approaches throw light on the Caribbean reality? It is quite evident that the Christian message which was adopted in the European experience leans to the person-centered approach and so has permeated the entire western world, including the Caribbean. However, the cultural experience of our African and East Indian ancestors were largely different, leaning more towards the society-centered approach. These cultures are community-based cultures. The individual finds his/her meaning only in relation to the community. Families were largely extended-type families. For the black population in the Caribbean, their historical experience of deracination and separation from their family and their inability to enter into marital relationships on the sugar plantations, created a unique family situation subsequent to emancipation, the effect of which we suffer even today.

A look at some statistics in St. Lucia, for example, will help us understand the reality. In the year 2010 the Population and Housing Census data indicate that at least 90.2% of the St. Lucian population claims some allegiance to a Christian religious body. Catholics amount to 61.3 % of that population. In 2001, of the 2,788 births recorded, 2,369 were born out of wedlock (84.5%). In 2008, of the 2,210 births recorded, 1,867 were out of wedlock (84.5%). The number of marriages in those two years was 513 and 631 respectively. The quinquennial report sent to Rome in 1992 had this to say:

> In St. Lucia, the rate of married Catholic couples is on the increase, but still a shocking number, almost 88% of our children are born out of wedlock. Marriage is not an inherent tradition of our people. Hence the Marriage Encounter Movement struggles to encourage Catholic marriages to live out their vocation according to the teachings of the Church.[93]

Such figures are bound to raise many questions. Of course, the nuclear family structure is what is taught to be the ideal, but in reality the extended family structure still exists among the East Indian families and families of African descent. Such a situation is further challenged by the fact that the single parent families are on the rise today. Do those figures directly indicate the Christian maturity or immaturity of such a people? Or does it in any way indicate a difference in the Christian maturity of those who live in non-legal unions versus those who live in legal unions? Could the reasons for the high incidence of such unions be only the lack of commitment or because it is expedient for the couples? Could it be that the perception of Christian marriage in the mind of some of our Caribbean people still remains a thing of the

---

[93] Archdiocese of Castries Quinquennial Report sent to Rome, 1988-1992.

upper class – those who are more able to afford? Could it be that many enter and remain in relationships mainly for economic stability and viability? In the light of those realities could it be that we need to reassess the basis for making moral judgments on human experiences? These are just a few of the questions raised by the Caribbean family structure.

The answer to some of these questions may be rather unclear to us, but there is no doubt that there are positive principles of life like loyalty, responsible parenthood, strong kinship ties in the extended families, and a sense of community that are evident in some Caribbean families, that could be affirmed. For one thing, they would experience a Church which shows care instead of condemnation, one in which they can find a home. This is an attempt to understand people's lives and to create the space for dialogue with the Christian message while not condoning any sinful situation. That is evangelization and this is our task.

The Gender Issue - Homosexuality

Given the recent Supreme Court ruling in the United States of America,[94] it is not uncommon for people from the various walks of life to ask where does the Church stand on homosexuality, its orientation, activity and social structures within which it exists. In this contemporary milieu it seems impossible to avoid the issue as it is at the forefront of debates in many Caribbean islands and around the world as a social, political, human rights and moral issue.

On May 8, 2014, during their Annual Plenary Meeting held in Mandeville, the Bishops of the Antilles articulated a statement to address this issue. Its point of departure was the institution of marriage understood as the very cell of society and the Church life. Quoting the Second Vatican Council, the Bishops recognize that "Christ our Lord has abundantly blessed the love of man and woman, which is rich in divine love and modeled on Christ's own union with the Church."[95]

---

[94] On Friday, June 26, 2015, the United States Supreme Court ruled by a 5 to 4 majority vote that the Constitution guarantees a right to same-sex-marriage. mobile.nytimes.com/2015/06/27/us/supreme-court-same-sex-marriage.html?referrer-

[95] Austin Flannery, O.P. (Ed), *Vatican Council II*, Pastoral Constitution on The Church in the Modern World, 48.

However, the Bishops saw the need for the Church to reach out to our brothers and sisters who espouse a lifestyle that is contrary to the divine teaching proclaimed by the Church. We saw the need to affirm that they are loved and blessed by God with many gifts and talents which have enriched both Church and society.

The Bishops also recognized the pain, anguish and trials that those persons undergo, especially within the atmosphere that is prevalent in the Caribbean. Like Pope Francis, we hope that they will seek to know and love personally the will of God who embraces all his children, without exception, with a love that surpasses all understanding.

This is the basis of God's law and commandments which have as their objective the total fulfillment or happiness of persons. The Church recognizes the fact that God always reveals his designs for his creatures which are made in the very image of God (Gen. 1:27). When human beings begin to fathom the beauty of this teaching and how it impacts upon people's situation, it leads us to consider two aspects of God's revelation: Creation which determines the law of nature and Redemption or re-creation which pertains to the divine positive law consonant with the salvation and glorification of humanity.

It is evident from the species created that there is a set order that regulates and furthers the on-going creation set in motion by God, the Creator. Both inanimate and animate beings are regulated by a certain design that is enshrined in the very act of creation (cf. Gen. 1: 11-12; 24-25). Of interest is the fact that all are created according to their kind. Most importantly, "God created man in his image; in the image of God he created him: male and female he created them"(Gen. 1:27). They are created to complement one another and are explicitly directed to multiply and care for the earth (cf. Gen. 1:28). For believers—be they Jewish, Christian or Muslim—this creation story undergirds the essence of marriage and the family.

The Ten Commandments are the basics of the divine law, the objective of which is proper relationships with God and with fellow human beings. The Saviour sums up the Decalogue under the Great Commandment: love God and love neighbour (cf. Dt. 6: 4-5; Lev. 19: 17; Matt. 22:37-40), all of which culminates in the redemptive death and resurrection of Jesus, which ushers in a new life welling up into eternal life. This Great Love Story of salvation could be considered as God embracing all of humanity with an everlasting love. Dare we say that married love between man and woman reflects this beautiful union?

By his saving death and glorious resurrection, Jesus has liberated humankind from the innumerable burden of laws and regulations which were meant to safeguard God's covenanted relationship with mankind. However, in no way was license intended, as St. Paul reminds the early Church: *"My brothers, you were called, as you know, to liberty; but be careful, or this liberty will provide an opening for self-indulgence. Serve one another, rather, in works of love"* (Gal. 5:13). Clearly St. Paul gives us an indication of our relationships with one another, a relationship that is based on love that is Christ-related.

Having established the context, within which Christians should conduct themselves, be they married or single, we wish to comment on the topical issue of gender. It must be clearly established that all human beings, be they male or female, young or old, are endowed with inalienable rights, but these rights must not infringe upon the rights of other human beings nor undermine the common good of society. What are some of those rights? The right to freedom of expression, right to freedom of religion, right to marry and to have a family, the right to an education, health care, housing, and employment. Without such rights life would not be worth living!

Above all, the right to life is the most fundamental of all rights; all others are predicated on that right to life that ensures the integrity of one's dignity which is imparted neither by Church nor State, but by God, the Creator. Each person, male or female, is equal in the pursuit of those rights that ensure fulfillment of one's potential, but it must be remembered that with rights come responsibilities. For Christians, such responsibilities entail their relationship with God, and are expressed by acts of reverence, respect, and acceptance of God's will which is enshrined both in natural and divine positive laws. No one has a right to contravene natural and divine laws because doing so leads to our peril and deterioration of family life and society.

Within the context of gender, homosexual relationships also challenge the institution of marriage, as occurred in the USA on June 26, 2015. World-wide there is much discussion with a view to altering the age-old traditional definition thus having far-reaching implications for family-life and kinship, civil society and the Church. Marriage between one man and one woman is not only a Christian institution. It is also pre-Christian and is recognized as the ideal means and context whereby children are raised with love that is both masculine and feminine [to correspond to the masculinity and femininity of each person], and educated for their rightful role in the society. Christ himself recognized and raised this complementary union of man and woman to the level of a sacrament—not just as a contract but a covenant. We never tire to reflect on this marital union as one that signifies the great mystery of covenanted union of Christ and his Church (cf. Eph. 5: 21-33).

One of the "rights" being promulgated aggressively today in the Caribbean Region is the union between persons of the same sex. Notwithstanding our age-old tradition of marriage that ensures the propagation of the human race and the promulgation of our civilization and culture, same-sex unions are being promoted by very powerful forces, as a "civil right" and an alternative form of "marriage." In reality "Legal recognition of homosexual unions or placing them on the same level as marriage would mean not only the approval of deviant behaviour, with the consequence of making it a model in present-day society but would obscure basic values which belong to the common inheritance of humanity. The Church cannot fail to defend these values, for the good of men and women and for the good of society itself."[96]

Given the fact that assets are jointly owned by persons espousing such a union, the Church recognizes

---

[96] *Considerations Regarding Proposals to Give Legal Recognition to Unions Between Homosexual Persons,* Guidelines from the Congregation for the Doctrine of the Faith 2003, Section 11.

the justice issue thus entailed. Nonetheless, in this regard the Church's teaching remains clear: "Nor is the argument valid according to which legal recognition of homosexual unions is necessary to avoid situations in which cohabiting homosexual persons, simply because they live together, might be deprived of real recognition of their rights as persons and citizens. In reality, they can always make use of the provisions of law like all citizens from the standpoint of their private autonomy to protect their rights in matters of common interest. It would be gravely unjust to sacrifice the common good and just laws on the family in order to protect personal goods that can and must be guaranteed in ways that do not harm the body of society."[97]

Does that mean that the Church is not concerned about men and women having such an orientation? Of course not! The Church's role is to proclaim the Truth, "in season, out of season" (Cf. 2 Tim. 4:2) to each and every person who would listen to the Word of God being proclaimed. It is that proclamation received in faith that will bring about a deeper understanding of the Truth that the Holy Spirit wishes to impart to every human being in

---

[97] *Considerations Regarding Proposals to Give Legal Recognition to Unions Between Homosexual Persons*, Guidelines from the Congregation for the Doctrine of the Faith 2003, Section 9.

the quest of happiness and peace. Hopefully that deeper understanding will lead to a true encounter with Christ for all of us so that we see in each other brothers and sisters on the way to Christ. However, when people make choices for lifestyles contrary to the gospel, the Church must be full of mercy, slow to judge. Rather She proclaims "in season, out of season," the love and compassion of the Good Shepherd who tenderly seeks out the stray sheep and says to one and all: "*Come to me, all who labour and are overburdened*" (Matt. 11:28).

Therefore, in imitation of the Good Shepherd, the Church must care for all human beings and love them. All are God's creatures "made in the image of God." To that end, the Church teaches regarding homosexual, bisexual and transsexual orientations: "They must be accepted with respect, compassion, and sensitivity. Every sign of unjust discrimination in their regard should be avoided. These persons are called to fulfill God's will in their lives and, if they are Christians, to unite to the sacrifice of the Lord's Cross the difficulties they may encounter from their condition" (CCC, #2358).

The mission of the Church is clearly defined: "*Go, therefore, make disciples of all the nations; baptise them in the name of the Father and of the Son and of the Holy Spirit, and teach them to observe all the commands I give you*" Matt. 28:19-20a). That's the Church's mandate: to proclaim the Good News of salvation!

Therefore, we appeal to our Catholic faithful to stand firm in the faith handed on to us by the One, Holy, Catholic and Apostolic Church impelled by and committed to the teaching and mission of Jesus. We also strongly urge that all will respect those brothers and sisters of ours who admit to having an orientation different from the majority of our people. We must respect them, do no violence to them, and respect their basic human rights, for they, along with us, are made in the image and likeness of God.

Respect for others, however, does not imply approval of the life styles contrary to the traditional ones. Even if the State were to decriminalize the anti-buggery law, one must always bear in mind that legality does not make a thing moral. Our duty, under all circumstances, is to express love and concern as we remain firm in the faith of our Fathers fostered and maintained by God's Holy Spirit.

Summary

All the topics raised in the foregoing discussions are merely a scratch on the surface of what is worthy of much more thorough research and exposition. These have been raised to facilitate a focus into the Caribbean reality which is viewed against the Christian Gospel, thereby seeking to articulate what can be termed a Christian civilization. That civilization, to my mind, is not to be perceived as an end in itself, or a stage at which we eventually arrive. It is to be perceived rather as a continuous process of maturation to bring ourselves as a people to a more wholesome sense of our humanity. Therefore, such a process will, of necessity, take certain shapes and postures on the physical, psychological, historical, socio-economic and cultural levels.

First of all, we need to own our history. As hard as this may sound, it is always the first step to liberation. In order to promote a civilization of being, we have to acknowledge who we are; that is, grow into a deeper acceptance of what we have been, embrace what we are, and chart the course for a more positive future. It is not a call to shoulder-patting or to tell how good a job our predecessors have done. It is a necessity for making positive psychological movements or shifts from one stage of existence to another. Let me use the Exodus experience to illustrate my point. That experience for the Israelites consisted of three movements: bondage, liberation and covenant relationship. Israel's experience of bondage was real and painful and historical, but became a moment in the process of salvation only when it was personally acknowledged and accepted. Bondage alone leads to nothing; however, bondage acknowledged opens the way to salvation. Before we can reach the stage of covenant relationship with God, which is the climax of the Christian experience, so to speak, we must seek to eradicate all forms of bondage in our psyche by first acknowledging it.

Secondly, if the Caribbean Church is to be a genuine promoter of that civilization She has to be endowed with certain qualities:

1. She has to be perceived and experienced as a Church of compassion, on the pattern of the divine Master. Historically, Caribbean people have not always experienced that quality in its totality at the hands of the Church; especially those of the lower class. They have seen it as an institution which is quicker to condemn their way of life than to encourage them onto a higher level of being. The Church must always be the first to give a sense of comfort and welcome to its people.

2. She has to be perceived and experienced as a therapeutic community; being more acceptable to its members, especially in their struggles. To seek always to create a sense of being a home to which every person feels that he/she belongs. The Church should

never be experienced as alienating to its members, especially the poor. Its ministry ought to be designed in such a way as to facilitate full participation of all members. It must be experienced as a place where gifts are nurtured and shared. That sense of being at home with the Church could certainly help in eradicating some of the superstitions that exist in the very fabric of the lives of a significant number of our people.

3. She has to be perceived and experienced as a dialoguing Church; a people who can live with differences; one that is open to accept truth in others, and being comfortable to work with them. This leads to the inevitable promotion of ecumenical inter-religious dialogues. It is not to be seen simply as an accommodated extra, but an intrinsic dimension of being Church today. The quest for unity even from the biblical standpoint does not mean uniformity. Diversity is not an enemy to unity because it only comes to its full stature in collaborative effort. The Church has to pattern what she teaches in that regard.

4. Liberation always involves growth and coming to self-hood – a process of incarnation or inculturation. The Caribbean as a people needs to be more and more aware of the fact that we have a unique contribution to make to the world. It is a contribution that only we can

make by being Caribbean, with all our background and experiences. Therefore, our theology, Christology and Ecclesiology will carry some unique features because their context is Caribbean. Our liberation has to truly come from within and then our celebration, our liturgy, will inevitably reflect liberation with its language and forms. True liberation always boosts a people's sense of dignity and self-respect which are perfect Caribbean principles.

5. The Church will need to be perceived and experienced as having a prophetic voice, that is, one which upholds justice for all and promotes the rights of every human person. To be otherwise would be contradictory to the Christian message. Its leadership must be perceived and experienced as persons who are ready to put their lives on the line for the rights of their people. It is the only way that we can have a voice that is authentic, and can at the same time be a source of inspiration to the political and economic structures. Such a position requires a great deal of vigilance in keeping abreast with issues which challenge the lives of those whom we serve.

6. In light of this responsibility to justice, the Caribbean Church of the future will need to pay particular attention to women who, in fact, form the major sector of its membership. There is no doubt that in the Caribbean,

women in the Church and in other institutions have suffered innumerable indignities because they are women. In a male-dominated Church and society, they have been subjected to a role of 'faithful servant' without any serious recognition of their true status or function. This issue cannot be left unattended if we are to make a significant and meaningful step into the future. They constitute the main stream of the Church's life and witness, and form the back-bone of many Caribbean families. Therefore, their recognition as formators of society has to go beyond mere tokenism to a sense of equality of participation in the development of Church and nation.

However, to sustain a liberation mentality and disposition in the Caribbean, there is need for a certain sense of vigilance against some of the threats to the liberation process. The first of these threats is the subtle introduction of neo-colonial mentalities. It is lamentable even to think that racial and colour discrimination and prejudices are still very present among us in all forms. Working towards their eradication must remain on our agenda. Class differences still pose a great challenge to the desired balance in our society and have, of necessity, to remain the concern of the Christian community. More overt, however, is an ethic of individualism, materialism, and consumerism, which is sweeping the Caribbean world. The soap opera mentality of overnight success needs to be seen as negative because it is not realistic. It encourages abuses of every kind and constantly presents to the Caribbean mind a false view of success, and therefore, a false view of true liberation.

Finally, the way to true liberation of the mind is through education – wholesome formation of persons; that is, to feed the mind with the best information that would make for good living. Not simply information for its own sake, but that which will make for an integral development of the human person. It will involve the assimilation of appropriate means of human communication, knowledge to appreciate technologies and sciences, knowledge of the art of working collaboratively, acquisition of values of respect for every person and all persons and nature, methods of praying and strategies for spiritual development, knowledge of the Holy Scriptures and its application to our lives, and ultimately seeking the knowledge of God – the ultimate fulfillment of mankind.

I end with these words from Dr. Martin Luther King Jr., quoting an eloquent poet in his speech entitled *The Great March to Freedom*. It reads:

Fleecy locks and black complexion cannot forfeit nature's claim.

Skin may differ but affection dwells in black and white the same.

Were I so tall as to reach the pole, or to grasp the ocean at a span,

I must be measured by my soul; the mind is the standard of the man.[98]

Caribbean Theological Conference, St. Lucia, June 1994

---

[98] Dr. Martin Luther King Jr. in his speech: *The Great March to Freedom*, Detroit, June 1963.

POSTSCRIPT

A Theological Reflection on "Bamboo Bursting" in the Caribbean

The word cannon very often rings an uncomfortable sound in the ears of many people because of the close association with the word artillery. Before the introduction of the word cannon into the military vocabulary in the 1400s, the word artillery was common. It is loaded with meanings that connote warfare, destruction, revenge, murder, and even the more palatable word of self-defense.

In St. Lucia, the military might of those who shaped our colonial past is evident in the ruins of many strategic points which today have turned out to be places of relaxation, scenic beauty and tourist attractions. Could it be true the words of the prophet Isaiah have been fulfilled among us? That "*these will beat their swords into ploughshares, their spears into pruning hooks, nations will not lift up sword against nation, there will be no more training for war?*" (Isaiah 2:4). For our purposes here these words of Isaiah could be paraphrased thus: "*those cannons of war and defense today in our land are silent.*"

But there are other cannons which ring a different tune, a tune of announcement, recognition, and honour. It has become customary in our tradition that persons of great honour and importance who visit our shores receive the gun salute. This we might say is synonymous with the sound of the cannon. The same happens at the death of a publically recognized person. The booming sound commands a silence which in an instant calls to mind the importance of the one who is mourned. Essentially, it says to an honourable figure, "I salute you." From ancient times until now, this has been the privilege of kings and persons of such high estate to be saluted in such manner on pastoral visits to their "kingdom."

Christmas, as Christians understand it, is a visitation - that of a Great King and Lord, our Saviour Jesus Christ. He comes among us as the King of all Kings and cultures around the world have developed varied ways of welcoming and saluting Him on His birthday. In the Caribbean we have the tradition of the Bamboo cannon as a messenger or herald the coming of Christmas. The "firing" reverberates through the hills and valleys, making it known that someone great is coming and is worthy of our attention and celebration.

"Bamboo Bursting in the Caribbean"

The cannon is made of a single piece of bamboo about five or six feet in length and six to eight inches in diameter. The "gun-powder" for the cannon is kerosene. The cannon is usually set on a piece of wood so that the mouth is raised off the ground. Then the kerosene is poured in the small hole at the bottom. The kerosene fumes cause the ignition. When the fumes are ignited the resulting boom can be heard from a great distance. After repeated ignitions and booming, the kerosene gets hotter and consequently produces a progressively louder blast.

It is important to note, too, that this activity goes on throughout the season of Advent. It is a time of preparation, a time of waiting, a time of renewing. The scripture readings chosen for the liturgical celebrations during the period reaffirm that spirit of preparation and renewal. Physical preparations are made with a festive mood as to celebrate the birthday of a King; but the spiritual preparation takes the mind and heart of the Christian beyond the mere physical and also focuses on the ultimate coming of Jesus as judge of the world. The words of the prophet Isaiah put it across beautifully when he says:

> A voice cries, Prepare in the wilderness a way for the Lord. Make a straight highway for our God across the desert. Let every valley be filled in, every mountain and hill be laid low, let every cliff become a plain, and the ridge a valley; then the glory of the Lord shall be revealed and all mankind shall see it; for the mouth of the Lord has spoken (Isaiah 40:3-5).

"Bamboo Bursting," as we know it, has a heralding function in the folk ways of St. Lucia, Dominica and other islands in the Caribbean.[99] It tells of the joyful hope that Christians have of the coming of our Saviour Jesus Christ. Its booming effect is not an announcement of

---

[99] In Guyana, for example, theirs is not a pre-Christmas tradition, but a similar welcome is given to dignitaries including the Roman Catholic Bishop during his pastoral visit to the Amerindian communities in the interior of this South American territory. In Trinidad, on the other hand, bamboo bursting is used to herald the approach of the Divali season, which is the Festival of Light in the Hindu community.

war, but rather one of love and peace. This is the message of Christmas. A message that comes with the effect of beating swords into ploughshares, spears into pruning hooks, and gives us no reason to train for war. This is Christmas in true Caribbean style. Unfortunately, a tradition which, in the advent of the cell phone, the iPod and other forms of electronic media is slowly being shifted from the minds of the young for whom this was also a form of pre-Christmas entertainment.

ABOUT THE AUTHOR

Bishop Gabriel Malzaire was born at Mon Repos in St. Lucia, on October 4, 1957. His formal theological education consists of a BA in Theology from the University of the West Indies, St. Augustine (1984), MA in Theology from the Catholic Theological Union in Chicago (1989), Licentiate and Doctorate in Systematic Theology from the Pontifical Gregorian University in Rome (1996-2000).

His work experience included, teaching at the Mon Repos Combined School (1975–1979); assistant parish priest, Our Lady of the Assumption Parish, Soufriere, St. Lucia (1985–1987); assistant director of the Archdiocesan Pastoral Centre and Assistant Parish Priest of the Good Shepherd Parish at Babonneau in St. Lucia (1989–1992); Parish Priest of St. Lucy's Parish, Micoud, St. Lucia (1992–1993), lecturer at the Regional Seminary, Trinidad (1993–1996 and 2000–2002), apostolic administrator of the Diocese of St. John's-Basseterre, Antigua/Leeward Islands and the British Virgin Islands (2007–2012); and bishop of the Diocese of Roseau from 2002 to the present time.

His publications include, "Towards a Caribbean Christian Civilization," *Theology in the Caribbean Today:*

Perspectives (1994); Pastoral Letter on Reconciliation (2004); Pastoral Letter on the Eucharist (2005); Pastoral Letter on Catholic Education in the Territory of the Antilles Episcopal Conference (2011); *A Decade of Grace* (2012) and *Eucharist & The Poor* (2014). He was a regular columnist for the Catholic Chronicle newspaper of the Archdiocese of Castries (1989–1996).

In 2006, Bishop Malzaire was awarded the title "Man of the Year 2005" by the leading newspaper of Dominica, "The Chronicle," in its issue of 6 January 2006.

On the occasion of the celebration of the twenty-seventh anniversary of its independence in 2006, the government of Saint Lucia awarded him the Saint Lucia Medal of Honour (Gold) SLMH for eminent service toward the growth and development of the church.

The church in the Caribbean stands at a decisive point in its history and must of necessity decide what path it will take. It stands at the crossroads of either continuing along the same path or taking a more creative road by deepening the tradition that we have received in both theological reflection and in pastoral practice. Bishop Gabriel Malzaire, in these essays, pushes us towards and points us to the more rigorous path of incarnating our theology, spirituality and pastoral practice within the particularity of the Caribbean experience. He raises pertinent issues with reference to Jesus Christ, the Church and Christian Ethics. What is at stake, according to Bishop Malzaire, is the continued relevancy, authenticity and fidelity to the mandate of evangelization given by Jesus Christ to his disciples. I hope that these issues will stimulate greater reflection and discussion so as to bring to birth a church that is, "… incarnated…contextual…Caribbean."

Fr. Nigel J. Karam
Doctoral Student in Theology, Angelicum, Rome

Bishop Malzaire looks at the diversity of the Christian experience as the teachings of Jesus of Nazareth spread through a wide range of human cultures and ethnic groups and he follows its journey to the Caribbean. He reviews the latest scholarship on the nature of Jesus Christ in the Black Church and Christ and ethnicity in the Caribbean. While doing this, he raises bold and novel questions about how a religion that emerged through one of the most oppressive and exploitative histories of humanity, has adapted itself to the realities of the modern Caribbean. Bishop Malzaire highlights those years following Vatican II, in the 1960s and 1970s, as a key period of transformation. His book heralds this as a transformation both of the church and the people whom it serves: communities and congregations who increasingly take charge of molding an image of Christ and His Word that speaks to their needs and the collective consciousness of the Caribbean people.

Dr. Lennox Honeychurch
Historian, Commonwealth of Dominica

CPSIA information can be obtained at www.ICGtesting.com
Printed in the USA
LVOW08s2259080715

445421LV00001BB/1/P